90° in the Shade

T0307937

A psychograph of the South — a paradox of unrest in a land of contentment.

90°
IN THE SHADE

CLARENCE CASON

90° in the Shade

Clarence Cason

Illustrated by J. Edward Rice

Introduction by Bailey Thomson

THE UNIVERSITY OF ALABAMA PRESS
Tuscaloosa

Copyright © 1935 by The University of North Carolina Press
First Paperbound Edition Published 1983 by The University of Alabama Press
Introduction Copyright © 2001 by The University of Alabama Press
Tuscaloosa, Alabama 35487-0380
All rights reserved
Manufactured in the United States of America

2 4 6 8 9 7 5 3 1
02 04 06 08 09 07 05 03 01

Typeface: AGaramond

∞

The paper on which this book is printed meets the minimum requirements of
American National Standard for Information Science–Permanence of Paper
for Printed Library Materials, ANSI Z39.48-1984.

Library of Congress Cataloging-in-Publication Data

Cason, Clarence, 1896–1935.
90° in the shade / Clarence Cason ; illustrated by J. Edward Rice ;
introduction by Bailey Thomson.
p. cm.
Originally published: Chapel Hill : University of North
Carolina Press, c1935.
Contents: It never snows — Shadows of the plantation — Garlands of
straw — Pulpit and pew — Politics as a major sport — Fascism: Southern
style — Black figures in the sun — The machine's last frontier — They are
not all monsters — The philosopher's stone.
ISBN 0-8173-1107-6 (pbk. : alk. paper)
1. Southern States—Race relations. 2. Southern States—Social life
and customs—1865– 3. Southern States—Social conditions—1865–1945.
4. African Americans—Southern States—Social conditions—20th century.
I. Title: Ninety degrees in the shade.

F215 .C27 2001
975'.04—dc21
00-054481

British Library Cataloguing-in-Publication Data available

INTRODUCTION

Bailey Thomson

Clarence Cason came home to Alabama in 1928 to teach at the state university and to write about his native region. He belonged to that restless generation of southern intellectuals who, between the world wars, questioned the South's stubborn traditionalism, even as they tried to explain and defend its distinctiveness. From his professorial perch in Tuscaloosa, Cason wrote polished essays for leading national publications while contributing weekly editorials for newspaper readers. As a journalist in academia, he cultivated a broad audience for his eloquent though tentative observations about the "character" of a region that seemed to be a separate province.

In 1935, Cason collected his thoughts in a small book of essays titled *90° in the Shade.* In it, he declared that climate and the relaxation afforded by field and stream had given southerners excellent reasons for their notorious laziness. Still, he wrote, one could see "there is much work that ought to be done below the Potomac." He offered a modest prescription for reform, calling for a "quiet revolution" in politics and race relations.

Just days before the book's publication, however, Cason killed himself. He left no explanation, but apparently he feared angry reaction from fellow citizens to his mild criticisms and gentle suggestions. With his self-destruction, he epitomized the tortured southern intellectual, and many people later would associate Cason with another tragic figure from this period, W. J. Cash of North Carolina. Indeed, Cash in his *Mind of the South* shared Cason's fascination with the cotton mill industry and the region's peculiar politics. But Cash's suicide in 1941 on the heels of his book's critical success was the result of mental illness and not fear of rejection, as appears to have been the case with the Alabamian.

In 1983, the University of Alabama Press reprinted Cason's book, with an introduction by Professor Wayne Flynt of Auburn University. The distinguished historian noted how Cason had turned his literary gifts to capturing the pathos of race relations and other persistent problems. For example, Cason declared that the abominable practice of lynching would end when the so-called best people of the South risked their personal and commercial standing to denounce it.

This second reprint edition allows a new generation of readers to enjoy Cason's writing, not so much for any remedy he proposed but rather for the open-minded and loving way in which he addressed the region's tragic experience. He drew upon the objectivity of social science, but he wrote with the grace of an impressionist. The result was journalism that his intellectual heirs may emulate for the beauty of its language and the depth of its questions.

As a journalist and professor myself, I often wonder what Cason would say about Alabama today, as it begins the twenty-first century. What work remains undone in our time? Where have we been lazy to the detriment of our children's future? Is there still a distinctive southern culture, even as science has provided relief from the climate and endemic diseases? I shall offer a few thoughts on those questions, but first let us briefly examine Cason's career and his contributions to southern thought and letters.

Clarence Cason was born in Ragland, Alabama, on December 20, 1896, and grew up in Talladega, where his father, Eugene P. Cason, practiced medicine. From observing his father's practice, the boy learned how difficult life could be for Alabama's poor whites and blacks, many of whom lacked the money to pay for the services. "Experiences of this kind do not constitute scientific data," the son later wrote. "But they clutch the heart."

Young Cason also witnessed firsthand how lynching occurred even in communities that considered themselves "cultured." One morning as he made his way to Sunday school, he saw men dump a body at the courthouse. Later, Sunday school went forward as

Cason was born in 1896 and grew up in Talladega, Alabama, where he first encountered the evil of lynching. (Courtesy of Jane Simpson)

usual, and the boy heard not a word about the crime. Thus, he learned that the lynching problem ran much deeper in southern society than sporadic mob violence.

Cason followed his father to the University of Alabama. Fellow students remembered the slightly built young Cason as a dreamy poet who favored flashy clothes and answered to the nickname "Chico." He immersed himself in the literary life of the campus. He joined the Blackfriars Club, where he studied acting with Hudson Strode, who was only a few years older but already had returned to teach at his alma mater. Cason's interests also gravitated to journalism, which he learned by working on student publications and doing stints during the summers for newspapers, including work in Washington with the *New York Times.*

Upon graduation in 1917, Cason took a reporting job with the *Birmingham News.* But the Great War soon sucked him and other members of his generation into its conflagration. He enlisted in the U.S. Army and became an expert in the use of the Vickers machine gun. He spent six months in France teaching at an aerial gunnery school.

Upon his discharge in February 1919, Cason worked for a string of newspapers, including the *Louisville Courier-Journal.* While in Louisville, he taught high school for a while and attended a theological seminary. Still not satisfied, he enrolled at the University of Wisconsin for graduate studies in English literature. He earned a master's degree and worked toward a doctorate while teaching journalism and literature. In 1925, he moved to the University of Minnesota, where he taught journalism as an assistant professor. Two years later, he married Louise Elliott Rickeman of Galena, Illinois.

During his stay in the North, Cason encountered prejudice toward southerners, as when one of his deans once asked him, "What seems to be the air of scholarship in the South—to sit on the front porch and drink lemonade?" Yet he also was exposed to the ideas of Willard Bleyer, a pioneer at Wisconsin in transforming journalism into an academic discipline. Unlike Bleyer, how-

Cason was graduated from the University of Alabama in 1917, where he was known as a dreamy poet and flashy dresser. His friends called him "Chico." (Courtesy of Jane Simpson)

ever, who pursued the history of newspapers and other scholarly contributions, Cason preferred creative work. In his essays and other writings, he combined an intense desire to explain the world with a poetic sensitivity.

In 1928, Dean Charles H. Barnwell at the University of Alabama persuaded Cason to return to the campus and organize a journalism department within the College of Arts and Sciences. The invitation included freedom to pursue whatever model of instruction that Cason deemed appropriate.

In that day, most newspapermen—and I emphasize the male gender because there were few female reporters—learned their craft on the job, as Cason had done. They typically advanced in the newsroom from clerk to cub reporter and then to more demanding tasks as writers and editors. At Alabama, Cason sought to impart his love of the liberal arts to his journalism students, whom he believed in educating rather than merely training for a vocation. He used the Socratic method to elicit thinking, and he did not impose his opinions upon his listeners. Typically, he would sit on the side of his desk, pipe in hand, and draw students into a conversation about the week's news or some topic he had assigned. He guided their work with thoughtful criticism. Gould Beech, who edited the student newspaper, the *Crimson-White,* and later became an editorial writer and political activist in Alabama, recalled, "He was always encouraging you to learn more, to find out more, not coming to conclusions until you knew all the facts."[1]

Cason quickly enjoyed the esteem of his students and colleagues. One reason was that he continued to work as a journalist himself. His essays appeared in leading intellectual journals such as the *Nation, Yale Review, Virginia Quarterly Review, Sewanee Review,* and *Outlook.* His pieces also appeared in the *New York Times Magazine,* the *Baltimore Sun,* and other prestigious newspapers. He contributed regularly to the editorial pages of the *Birmingham News,* even doing a summer stint to fill in for a vacationing writer. He was also in demand as a public speaker, and his comments attracted editorial attention. Such prodigious work inspired Grover Hall's *Montgomery Advertiser* to describe Cason as one of the "most brilliant and engaging thinkers in Alabama."[2]

As a writer, Cason leaned toward the progressive Regionalists, who under the inspiration of Howard W. Odum at the University of North Carolina advocated planning and other modern methods to address the South's problems. But Cason's criticisms of his region stopped short of ridiculing its customs. For example, he did not join the followers of H. L. Mencken in excoriating the South's churches for their provincialism. Rather, he saw them as helping to hold together their communities, particularly those in isolated rural areas. Likewise, he refrained from condemning racial segregation—a position that would have been a radical step for a southern liberal. Cason's arguments were carefully nuanced to support what he called "intelligent and conservative" attitudes on both sides of the color line. He condemned lynching and racial demagoguery—those barbaric practices associated with the region's common whites—while encouraging solidarity between blacks and the region's white aristocrats.

Cason also found much to admire in the work of the Agrarians at Vanderbilt, who often were at odds with the Regionalists' emphasis on economic development. In 1931, he wrote Donald Davidson at Vanderbilt that the group's recent book, *I'll Take My Stand,* was an artistic triumph. Nevertheless, Cason deplored how Davidson and his fellow authors had used agrarianism to string together essays that defended southern tradition. Their method put too much emphasis on making a living. "I wonder whether a somewhat industrialized South will not still retain many of the human traits which we revere as characteristic of our section," Cason wrote.[3]

In 1934, Cason contributed a chapter to *Culture in the South,* published by the University of North Carolina Press and edited by the press's director, W. T. Couch. In the spring of that year, Cason wrote Couch, "I have had this little volume in mind in all the essays I have attempted on Southern subjects during the last six years."[4] The result was to be Cason's *90° in the Shade.* Many of the ideas would be distilled from Cason's previously published essays, but the author also expanded upon his interpretations and received many suggestions from Couch.

The two men exchanged enthusiastic letters about the project. Yet as the publication date neared, Cason grew somber and fearful that his criticism of the region, no matter how gently offered, might antagonize his fellow southerners. "I am convinced that it will be exceedingly difficult for me to remain in Tuscaloosa after the book is published," the author wrote on May 4, 1935.[5]

Earlier that day, he had sent an urgent telegram to Couch, warning that the book's dust jacket drew an unfortunate comparison to Carl Carmer's controversial *Stars Fell on Alabama,* which had portrayed The University of Alabama as being little concerned with intellectual life. Couch sought to calm his writer by suggesting he was simply suffering from "extreme nervousness." Cason's book combined good writing with straight thinking, and it would be a success, Couch predicted. "If I were in your place, I would go fishing and forget the whole thing."[6]

About this time, James Saxon Childers, literary editor of the *Birmingham News,* interviewed Cason at the author's home and found him "frightfully worried." Childers sought to assuage his fears by mapping out a campaign to assure a good reception for the book. Following the interview, Childers wrote a favorable article for his Sunday edition and sent a copy to Cason for his inspection. The next morning, Childers learned that Cason had shot himself on the previous evening, May 7, in his office at the Journalism Department. Cason's wife found him slumped on a chair, with an automatic pistol nearby.

Speaking for a shocked campus, President George Denny, in his comments to the *Tuscaloosa News,* declared, "[Cason] was one of the finest members of our faculty, a brilliant teacher and leader in his field of work."[7] Meanwhile, Couch informed the *News* that Cason's death was the result of "temporary unbalance caused by worry." The press would have halted publication had its editors known of Cason's mental state.[8]

Later, in a private letter, Couch confided to Jonathan Daniels, editor of the *Raleigh News and Observer,* that Cason had no reason to fear adverse reaction in Tuscaloosa: "I have never read any book about the South that I thought was written with better humor and was less likely to arouse antagonism." The book editor described Cason as a "quiet, gentle, retiring person who abhorred controversy. At the same time he was aware of the need for honest frank discussion."[9] In a letter to Hudson Strode, Couch wrote, "I am afraid I can never forgive [Cason] for wiping out a talent that in my opinion is so rare as to be almost non-existent."[10]

Still, Cason's fears were not entirely imaginary. The year before his death, a professor from Alabama College at Montevallo had an encounter with Tuscaloosa's Ku Klux Klan when about forty hooded members searched his car. This incident caused John Temple Graves II to write, "We don't blame Tuscaloosa for being afraid but the thing they have to fear is not Communism. It is Ku Klux-ism, lynching Moron-ism."[11] Meanwhile, Merlin N. Hanson claimed he had been fired from the *Mobile Register* a year earlier for writing in a Philadelphia magazine about people of mixed racial heritage. Cason may have overreacted, Hanson concluded, but he had written truthfully "about a section that carries its feelings around on the end of its nose."[12]

Despite such prickly sensitivity to criticism, local reaction to Cason's book was positive. A reviewer for the *Tuscaloosa News,* who was himself a scion of a prominent Black Belt family in Greensboro, found nothing offensive. The late author had drawn his conclusions fairly and did not seek to sensationalize the South, Hamner Cobbs concluded. "He wrote [his book] as a liberal critic who, loving the South, nevertheless hoped to contribute in his own modest way to its progress, who might help in stirring it from its lethargy."[13] Meanwhile, the state's editorial pages mourned the loss of "Chico," as their writers affectionately called Cason.

Nationwide, Cason's book inspired reviews and notices in many

In the early 1930s, Hudson Strode and Clarence Cason enjoyed rising reputations as writers and teachers at the University of Alabama. Pictured from left: Strode, Therese Strode, unidentified friend, Cason, and Louise Cason. (Courtesy of Jane Simpson)

leading newspapers and periodicals. Daniels observed in the *Saturday Review* that the South needed more authors who could write so intelligently.[14] A reviewer for the *New York Times* thought Cason had been too easy on his section's sins, such as lynching and child labor.[15] By contrast, *Time*'s reviewer reported Cason had cast "his dissatisfied eye over the Southern scene, finds it on the whole down-at-the heel, lazy, complacent, resigned, ignorant, cynical, exasperating." The reviewer, speculating that fear of local reaction drove Cason to suicide, wondered, "Had he jeopardized a pleasant life for the doubtful fame of writing a controversial book?"[16] In response to *Time*'s review, a former student of Cason's, Charles Alldredge, wrote the editors, "The University of Alabama is narrow, I will admit, but both faculty and students appreciated Cason for what he was, the ablest of its teachers."[17]

What were the ideas that drew such attention to Cason and ultimately led him to suicide after he sought to "psychograph" this separate province of the United States? Cason wrote that two great elements conditioned southern culture.

The first was climate—specifically the dog days of summer that drove people to the shade or, better yet, to the fishing holes. This languor disinclined southerners to address the problems that plagued their region, such as disease, exhausted agriculture, and ignorance. How different southerners were in 1935 from, say, residents of Wisconsin, whose unpredictable and severe winters accustomed them to accept change and new ideas. Cold weather did not produce the kind of enervating effect upon northerners that sultry summers inflicted upon southerners, Cason argued.

The South's second great conditioning element, Cason wrote, was the presence of African Americans. At that time, about one in four southerners was black, and the South remained the great center of African American population in America, although migration was continuing to take blacks out of the region and into northern cities. Relatively few blacks could vote in Alabama and other Deep South states, having lost the franchise around the turn of

At Alabama, Cason combined teaching and writing in an active career. His essays appeared in many of the nation's leading magazines and journals. (Courtesy of Jane Simpson)

the century. Opportunities for education and advancement were pitifully few. Schools for black students typically were inadequate and well below the even modest levels of education afforded whites. "Quite aside from such abstract concepts as human freedom and justice, can the South longer afford to jeopardize its economic future by continuing to harbor various delusions which are calculated to keep so large a part of its population in poverty and ignorance?" Cason asked. He argued that white southerners had to make room for blacks to take their proper place as good citizens and productive workers.

These two elements—a hot climate and a large population of blacks—had made the South a different kind of place, Cason believed. Unfortunately, this separate province had demonstrated complacency and even hostility to progress.

And what were some of the consequences for failing to think and act in more progressive ways? For one, Cason argued, Alabama and the Deep South in 1935 labored under politics that offered more sport than leadership. Demagogues pitted the poor white against the poor black, thereby helping condemn both to marginal existence. Another result was that churches in the South, so powerfully present in every community, too often turned inward rather than addressing the social problems at their doorsteps. Finally, Cason wrote, Alabama in the 1930s was not ready for the next wave of industrialism. It still offered cheap and docile labor at a time when America was becoming the technological leader of the world. The South's challenge was not the exploitation of workers in the mills and mines, although such incidences did occur. Rather, the question was "whether the introduction of new machines will not gradually remove the necessity for any kind of unskilled labor—children, women, or men."

Let us now turn the clock forward to our own time. How have Clarence Cason's observations fared?

Obviously, Cason underestimated the power of air conditioning to transform the Deep South after World War II. He even sounded silly when he predicted southerners would reject artificial cooling, preferring to let the summer heat remain a "welcome ally in that it makes the inside of houses and offices agreeably uninviting, if not actually prohibited territory." Once air conditioning tamed its summers, the South made its sunny climate a great selling point for attracting immigrants and new industries. After all, who cares about one-hundred-degree weather if one feels it only while racing from an air-conditioned Mercedes to a glass, air-conditioned office?

But what about race? Does it not continue to condition southerners at every level?

Yes, it remains a divisive, difficult issue, but hardly one that is confined to the Deep South. Many of the racial problems Alabamians and other southerners confront today are similar to those of say, New York, Illinois, or even Wisconsin. I think Cason would be astounded at how racial relations have improved in Alabama. Black citizens now have equal access to public education and other public facilities. They hold legislative, municipal, and county offices. And while acts of racism persist, there is no longer systematic terror of our black citizens by hooded murderers and lynch mobs. We know from the hindsight of experience that racial attitudes can be remarkably amenable to positive change, given sufficient determination at the federal level to enforce legal equality. Cason's generation of liberal southerners did not have such experience to guide them in assessing white southerners' attitudes. Instead, they saw what appeared to be an intractable allegiance to white supremacy, as reflected not only in Jim Crow laws and state constitutions but also in the folkways of the region. Under such conditions, they argued that the best solution was to make "separate but equal" true in its full meaning, rather than in terms of segregation alone.

So if climate no longer impedes our progress and race has become less of a southern issue and more of a national one, what elements condition the Deep South's culture today? Moreover, what deficiencies keep Alabama and some of its neighbors at or near the bottom in comparisons of income, education, and health? Of note, the South's distinctiveness continues to be argued in both positive and negative ways even today, just as it was in Cason's time.

If I may step into Cason's role for a moment and examine our native state of Alabama, I suggest that one important "conditioning element," to use his term, is the tension between persistent rural values that have been shaped by farm and town for generations and the emerging urbanization that is sprawling along the major interstates. By the end of the 1930s, for example, only about 30 percent of Alabamians lived in urban places. Today, 68 percent of the population is in the metropolitan areas. Pine trees now grow on former cotton fields, after farm families departed for urban jobs. In 1955, when I was a small boy growing up on a farm, our county had eighteen hundred cotton farmers. Now only three remain.

But even with this urbanization, we Alabamians—probably more than most Americans—value our traditions and cling to our old ways of thinking and acting. In some ways, this continuity is our strength. Alabama still feels like home to many of us who grew up here. We maintain our connections to country churches where our ancestors lie buried. We are still connected to large extended families, though we may not live so close to our relatives as did earlier generations. And many of us prefer to drive pick-ups even when we can afford nice automobiles.

But we Alabamians also have a nasty habit of ignoring social problems until some outside authority, such as the federal courts, forces us to pay attention. We remain inordinately suspicious of government and prefer that someone else pay for its services. And more recently, we have failed to plan adequately for suburban growth, deferring its cost by refusing to provide for necessary services such as roads, sewers, and schools. Within the last generation, Alabamians have seen constitutional reform, tax reform, and school reform wither at the hands of special interest bent on preserving the status quo. Yet the need for such reforms grows more intense with each passing year.

Our success or failure in resolving this tension between the pull of our rural past and the push of our urban present will determine what Alabama looks like in the year 2035—the one-hundredth anniversary of Cason's book. His call for a quiet revolution—one that would inspire a more realistic attitude about our problems and a determination to solve them—echoes though the decades to our own time. As in his day, we Alabamians cannot be content to lie in the shade, making excuses for our languor. We have too much work to do.

Notes

1. Interview with Gould Beech, Magnolia Springs, Ala., August 27, 1995.

2. *Montgomery Advertiser,* May 9, 1935.

3. Clarence E. Cason to Donald Davidson, June 4, 1931, Donald Davidson Papers, Special Collections, The Jean and Alexander Heard Library, Vanderbilt University. In another letter, Cason bemoaned how discussion of farming had degenerated into emphasis on making a living rather than pursuing a way of life. (Cason to Davidson, June 23, 1931, Ibid.)

4. Clarence E. Cason to W. T. Couch, May 29, 1934, in Academic Affairs: Records of the University of North Carolina Press, Author/Title Publication Records, Series 1, Cason, C. E., Ninety Degrees in the Shade, in University Archives, Wilson Library, University of North Carolina at Chapel Hill (hereafter RUNCP).

5. Cason to Couch, May 4, 1935, RUNCP.

6. Couch to Cason, May 6, 1935, RUNCP.

7. *Tuscaloosa News,* May 8, 1935.

8. W. T. Couch to N. G. Cobbs, May 8, 1935, RUNCP.

9. W. T. Couch to Jonathan Daniels, May 16, 1935, RUNCP.

10. W. T. Couch to Hudson Strode, July 26, 1938, RUNCP.

11. *Birmingham Age-Herald,* March 8, 1934.

12. Merlin N. Hanson, letter to the editor, *Time,* July 8, 1935, clipping in RUNCP.

13. Hamner Cobbs, "A Critical But Fair Study of Dixie," *Tuscaloosa News,* May 12, 1935.

14. Jonathan Daniels, "Southern Testament," *Saturday Review,* Vol. 12, No. 10 (July 6, 1935), 14.

15. C. McD. Puckette, "The South's Special Character," *New York Times Book Review,* May 19, 1935, 2.

16. "Warm South," *Time,* Vol. 25, No. 22 (June 3, 1935), 73.

17. Charles Alldredge, "Cason's Turmoil," letter to the editor, *Time,* July 8, 1935, clipping in RUNCP.

To the Memory of My Father

Air-conditioning cannot be a grand success in the South for the reason that the honest natives of the region recognize the natural summer heat as a welcome ally in that it makes the inside of houses and offices agreeably uninviting, if not actually prohibited territory.

It may be that ultimate truth lies in the spiritual attitude of many southerners who are always going fishing.

FOREWORD

Inasmuch as propriety requires that an author give fair warning as to what is to be met with in the pages of his book, I think that it would be well for me to begin by repeating a story.

My father was a physician who for more than twenty-five years fought such maladies as pellagra, malaria, and hookworm among the country people of the far South. One December night he drove sixteen miles into the hills to see a stricken family. The eldest son had walked the distance into town, and standing in the street before our house in the cold midnight, had called, "Hel-loo, Doc— hel-loo, Doc." When they reached the rough-pine cabin in the country, the doctor found the sallow-faced parents waiting by a smoking kerosene lamp in the sick room. Three children were huddled on a rumpled bed in a dark corner. Upon a pallet made of patched blankets and quilts, placed on the floor in front of a blazing fire of chestnut logs, a child lay unconscious from chills and fever. The doctor, in a despairing effort to make some pretense that would delay the pain of his announcement, took two five-cent coins from his pocket, placed them over the eyelids of the dying child, and moved his fingers gently through the moist hair. He knew that the parents would be comforted by these mysterious signs. Eight months later, the father walked stiffly into the doctor's office. "Been a-tryin' to save up and pay you off, Doc," he explained. "Anyways the preacher said fer me to jes' pace in here and git these two nickel pieces back to you. They's been a-botherin' of me."

Experiences of this kind do not constitute scientific data. But they clutch the heart. The impact of many such episodes upon a boy's consciousness serves to explain, as well as anything else could, the motive which underlies the present book.

For a southern man to set down an account of what he has observed in the South is not to imply that other scenes do not exist. If anyone is of a mind to match my illustrations with other pictures of a different hue, I shall not be greatly disturbed by that method of rejoinder, for at this moment I could do the same kind of thing myself. For instance, if in answer to my statements bearing upon the July heat in the southern region, someone should point out that the weather is cool in December, I have only to reply, "Quite so"—without in the least affecting the actualities of the summer temperature.

Half the triumph of Gamaliel Bradford's "psychographs" of human beings resides in that author's polite way of giving his readers a chance to answer back. He created the illusion of pleasant conversation among friends. He eschewed the jungle method of attempting to commit intellectual mayhem upon any of his listeners who might fail to share his opinions. His literary manner was housebroken and civilized. Not in Gamaliel Bradford, or Lytton Strachey either, does the reader find himself brought to earth and abruptly silenced by the dead weight of authenticity. Similarly, the "characters" deftly drawn by the seventeenth-century essayists bore no pretense of finality. Part of the fun of reading them must have been to disagree. Although John Earle in his *Whimsical Microcosmographic* wrote tartly of "A Mere Young Gentleman of the University" and delivered a pious tribute to "A Contemplative Man" who had educated himself, the understanding contemporary of that writer would hardly have regarded these two sketches as a premeditated argument against Oxford and Cambridge.

I am not sure whether it is possible to "psychograph" a part of the earth's surface, with its people and its physical background; but I thought there would be no harm in trying. Therefore I have drawn together some papers relating not primarily to the traits of selected human beings but to the characteristics of a part of the United States which is self-conscious enough and sufficiently insulated from the rest of the country to be thought of as a separate province. Thus it may be said that this volume constitutes a "character" of the southern states.

Foreword xxix

Henry J. Raymond, the founder of the New York *Times,* once complained against the public's insistence that a journalist must be partisan and consistent. "If those of my friends who call me a waverer could only know how impossible it is for me to see but one side of a cause," he remarked, "they would pity me rather than condemn me." If this annoyance at having to take a one-sided point of view is one of the tribulations of the newspaper commentator, the plight of other writers in this day and time is even worse, for if they profess no dogma voluntarily, the public is likely to hitch beliefs and purposes upon them. Therefore I embrace the privilege of stating that this book is not intended as a mere justification or condemnation of the South. At the risk of exhibiting myself as unmoral, I confess that I am far less interested in administering uplift in the southern states than in simply having the pleasure of talking about the region. And may I always be spared the vanity of hoping to be an influence.

Hearing the marvel that Stark Young and William Faulkner in their time have walked the same identical streets in Mississippi, one must avoid the feeling that he is compelled to choose between two irreconcilable social points of view. Stark Young and William Faulkner are not scientists; they write what is essentially art. Had they lived in Massachusetts or Indiana, one of them would still be a romanticist and the other a realist, and each would have taken his material where he found it. The England which bred Reynolds also produced Hogarth. Wherever men write stories or draw pictures, they put down what they see, and the result is neither mathematics nor sociology.

Much the same is true of the work of the essayist. He may think with pride that he, like the English country gentleman portrayed by Stephen Leacock, can leap upon his horse and ride freely and furiously in all directions. Still, how often can he be entirely certain that he is really prancing abroad on a brave steed and that he is not merely rocking on a hobby-horse in his own back yard? It would be a famous victory if an essayist could always be sure that his pronouncements are more than shadows cast by his own prejudices and predilections. But I am afraid that the laws of nature are ten to one that he in the end will have to admit, with Montaigne, that he himself is the groundwork of his book.

If all the South were like the Shenandoah Valley, only the promptings of Satan could stir the southern mind to discontent. Were it possible to regard Albemarle County, Virginia, as a microcosm of the South, then only an impish perversity could explain a southerner's dissatisfaction with the bounties of kind providence. But the plague of poverty—grim and deteriorating—has crept stealthily along the backroads in some of the other parts of the South. In a region blessed with abundant social and economic resources, the degrading effects of physical and mental privation upon a large part of the population can be attributed only to some gigantic error in philosophy, or to some overwhelming catastrophe. It may be that the Civil War constituted such a catastrophe, one from which the southern region can never expect to recover. Yet, in a yielding attitude of permanent hopelessness and complaint, there would be elements of defeatism and pusillanimous weakness which could have no appeal to southerners who prefer to look towards the rising sun.

Before the Civil War, the South demonstrated that, even on a continent already muddled by the hoarse cries of democracy, it was possible to rear a lofty culture upon the shoulders of a selected minority which was both able and responsible. Legalized slavery, the ante-bellum plantation, and the manor house of the Old South can never return. But shall we say the same of wisdom, dignity, and self-reliance?

The material and ideas composing this book have been simmering in the mind of the author for at least half a dozen years, and some of them have already overflowed into the pages of *The Virginia Quarterly Review, The Yale Review, The New York Times Magazine, The South Atlantic Quarterly, The Outlook and Indepen-*

dent, The Sewanee Review, the Baltimore *Evening Sun,* and *The North American Review.* Reprinted passages, however, in every case have been placed in a fresh context, and the greater portion of the present work is new.

The author's obligations, both direct and indirect, are manifold. To the staff of the University of North Carolina Press, he is indebted for invaluable guidance and evidences of warm human sympathy; to James Edward Rice, for his painstaking efforts to illuminate the text with his camera; to Hudson Strode, for friendly criticism of the manuscript; to William Hepburn, for his counsel and encouragement; to Lee Bidgood, for some recollections of a boyhood in tidewater Virginia; to Paul Terry and Verner Martin Sims, for two photographs made in connection with a project under their supervision; to Ronald Chalmers Hood, for collaboration on passages relating to the TVA; to Louise Cason, for patient assistance which far exceeded the bounds of the marriage vows; and to Jane, aged six, for the tender consideration which persuaded her to play quietly in her own room while her incomprehensible father sat long at his desk.

Clarence Cason
Tuscaloosa, Alabama
December 20, 1934

CONTENTS

90° in the Shade

Chapter I

It Never Snows

I

JAMES J. HILL, the railroad builder, studiously governed his investments in accordance with his business maxim that no man upon whom the snow does not fall is ever worth a tinker's dam. Such a conception implies no recommendation for the southern part of the United States. I can remember that during my boyhood in the deep South we used to be able to make snow ice cream once or twice a year. With a large kitchen spoon we would scoop the fresh snow from where it lay banked lightly on a railing of the garden fence and mix it in a bowl with cream, sugar, and vanilla extract. It made our palates tingle with exoticism. Our feeling was that little Rollo, whose fun at ice skating was described in our third-grade reader, would virtually subsist on snow ice cream should he take advantage of his opportunities in the cold North where he lived. But it has been snowing less and less in the South during the past thirty years, and as a consequence the country has no doubt gone to the dogs long since—from the point of view of Mr. Hill's philosophy.

Their English heritage restrains most Americans from thinking of geography except in terms of investments. Even so, there is one respect in which all must agree that

3

the change in the southern climate is not a calamity. A
certain kind of southerner can, by nature, be happy with
a hole in his pants. Other southerners have been forced
by necessity to cultivate the faculty. So it may be just as
well that the climate has been moderating. This lack of
concern for frayed trousers is in itself a conspicuous element in southern solidarity. Whether it constitutes a
regional virtue is another question, for, as Gertrude Stein
says, one may like a view and still prefer to sit with his
back to it.

Such a conception inevitably raises the disturbing possibility that southern complacency (another aspect of the
regional solidarity) may contain large doses of wishful
thinking. A poet from another part of the country, who
once surrounded himself with camellias and wistaria in
a southern town, was amazed when a native gentleman
of parts frankly advised him, for the sake of his career,
to get away before it was too late. Southern persons who
in their youth have cherished special aspirations experience no difficulty in understanding this advice. Do such
persons, after having realized that it is too late for them
to take their places in creative activities of the outside
world, simply try to compensate in the manner of spin-
sters who scoff at marriage, or in the vein of the members
of the Sew-We-Do Club who are saddened at the im-
moralities of the Society set, or in the manner of the
unsuccessful speculators who attempt to heap scorn upon

Wall Street? But that disturbing possibility must be admitted only parenthetically. Too much analysis of it would leave one mentally unbuttoned.

If snow falls infrequently on the southern land, the sun displays no such niggardly tendencies. In Mississippi there is justification for the old saying that only mules and black men can face the sun in July. Summer heat along the middle Atlantic coast and on the middle western plains causes more human prostrations than it does in the South. The difference lies partially in the regularity of high summer temperatures in the South but mainly in the way the southerner takes the heat. A Georgian takes the heat relaxed in a hammock or reclining on the bank of a shaded stream, wherein he has cast a hook for catfish, rather hoping that they will not disturb him too much. Golf in Georgia, Bobby Jones to the contrary notwithstanding, will never become more than measurably popular. It has the defect of not taking enough time. Fishing and hunting are better adapted to the native temperament. The most typical southern business man of my acquaintance is inclined to welcome rainy days because they enable him to get things in order at his real estate office. While the New Yorker or the Chicagoan rushes out into the heat of July and has a sunstroke, the southerner's discretion, which often persists throughout the winter, constitutes one of the conditioning elements of his unified culture.

2

There is no escaping the conviction that fishing in the South is pursued for its own sake, and not as a means of recuperation between business deals. No one is shocked because most of the cockroaches used for bait are obtained from grocery stores. Instead of being filled with alarm at the unsanitary conditions suggested by that fact, representative southerners would hardly demand a more noble service from grocery stores than the furnishing of cockroaches well bred with respect to size and degree of toughness. (They should be just large and tough enough to stay on a hook without being large and tough enough to prove formidable when handled.)

Although I know that it is heresy to suggest such an idea in the midst of an age of progress, it may be that ultimate truth lies in the spiritual attitude of the southerners who are always going fishing. A person who has achieved an immunity from the everlasting inner demand that he improve upon his earthly position must possess an unusual degree of cosmic equilibrium. He must have learned in some way that composure of the human spirit is all that actually matters. He has attained, without conscious effort, the serenity for which all men strive.

Activity, as he perhaps knows through some instinctive realization, is but a confession that peace is unendurable. It is in search of peace that all activity is directed. A parallel may be drawn from music. After a symphony of Brahms, it is the ensuing moment of silence into which the spiritual satisfaction of the hearer is mainly concentrated. One has the impression that all the sounds of the music were contrived in order to produce that single ecstatic moment of profound and complete satisfaction. If this analysis is sensible, one must feel occasionally that the sounds of music are arranged in such a way as to compose the soul and mind for the concentrated joy of a moment of silence, a vacant interval in time made perfectly endurable for the restless spirit of man.

It is much the same way with physical and mental activity. We build a fire in the grate in order that we may sit before it in comfort and ease. The fire in the grate is not the thing we want; it is the comfort and ease. Similarly, the principal joy of intellectual activity is involved in the attainment of a satisfactory conclusion, a moment in which the intellectual struggle gives way to a brief interval of serene comfort of the mind.

What shall we say of the person who is not influenced by the driving force which impels his fellows to improve upon the conditions about them? Shall we say that he is decadent or that he is the possessor of wisdom? Whatever the correct answer may be, the fact remains that no great consciousness of dissatisfaction can be in the minds of southerners who are forever going fishing. Without being under the necessity of forcing themselves through rounds of accomplishment, they can endure peace. Without having the refractory sounds of the universe resolved into a harmony for them, they can endure silence. No one should miss the significance of the fact that the old houses of Charleston have their blind sides turned towards the street.

At any rate, all men and women of consequence in the eastern part of the United States sail for Europe if they can as soon as the summer heat begins. In the South, however, the foreign tourist agencies know that their summer prospects lie chiefly with the school teachers. Persons of consequence in the South are satisfied to go fishing.

3

Upon the ethnic structure of the South the sparsity of snow has exerted a tremendous influence. It brought the Negro and has kept the Scandinavian away. When the first slave ships came three hundred years ago, it was natural for them to drop their African cargoes upon the warm soil of the cotton and rice plantations. During the three centuries of his residence in the southern states the Negro has had almost as much as the sunshine to do with conditioning the lives of the white people of the region. Like the heat of the sun, the Negro has delimited activity among the whites; like the sun, he has given his energy to the growing of crops for the white man. The floods of immigration which overwhelmed most of the United

One of the large homes in Tuscaloosa, on the edge of the Alabama black belt. The family residence of Robert J. Van de Graaff.

Family home of General William
Crawford Gorgas, on the campus
of the University of Alabama.

States for a generation after 1890 made little headway in the South, where the native populations, which had not completely succumbed to the doctrine of bigger towns at any cost, insisted that the South already had as many people as the Negroes could support.

When the presence of plenty of slaves allowed southerners to have a decent respect for the summer heat in building their residences, the characteristic form of regional architecture was developed. Wide hallways and high ceilings insured ample ventilation, and the custom of setting the kitchen off at one side relieved the drawing-room guests from the malodorous fumes of boiling cabbage and frying red snapper in August. With the passing of slavery and the arrival of the Spanish bungalow, however, the southerner more than ever began to feel under the compulsion to seek fresh air on the outside. It used to be said that travelers could always tell when they were in Virginia by the accumulation of dust under the hotel beds. Having recently spent a night at one of the immaculate hostelries of Richmond, I am sure that such a statement would be an arrant libel today. But it is true that the genuine southerner harbors a greater concern for his garden than for the inside of his house. It must be agonizing for southern publishers to realize that books cannot be read beside a cape jessamine bush in the moonlight. The New England fireside chair—from which one looks through the window upon the snow and ice of a long winter, and then takes down another volume from the bookshelves—has no counterpart below the Potomac. The southerner reads the morning newspaper because he wants to know about the Society events and the election campaigns, which he regards in somewhat the same light; but he thinks books are suitable only for invalids.

Nor is too much to be expected of air-cooling machines in the way of keeping southerners from spending most of their time out of doors. Air-conditioning cannot be a grand success in the South for the reason that the honest natives of the region recognize the natural summer heat as a welcome ally in that it makes the inside of houses and offices agreeably uninviting, if not actually prohibited territory.

Although it is true that the southern states are remarkable for the high percentage of their native-born population, no one should make the mistake of thinking that the social structure of the South as a whole is homogeneous. In no other part of the United States are class lines so rigidly drawn. One of the delights of my four years of residence in Wisconsin was the custom of going on numerous picnics in the late spring and early summer. Crossing the beautiful pasture lands of that state, we used to notice that the cows invariably faced in the same direction. It became a sort of byword with us. "All facing the same way," we would say to each other every time we sighted a herd of Guernseys. The farmers of that fine state, where the heavy snowfall brings the grass forth in succulent abundance every spring, also give the impression of going in the same direction on a basis closely approaching equality. But in the South it is a scientific fact, if a continuous observation of the phenomenon can be accepted as scientific evidence, that cows in the pasture do not face the same way; and it is an economic fact, so well established as to need no proof, that the farmers themselves are by no means going in the same direction.

The heavy snows of Wisconsin are influential in giving the farmers the kind of ambition which comes from physical vigor; also the snow plays a part in giving the cows plenty of grass to eat, and this results in their having a definite and obvious way of spending their time in the pasture. On the other hand, the long assault of the summer heat in the South is more effectual in baking the grass than the scarce winter snow can be in reviving it. As a consequence, the cows, mulling over the meadows, feel themselves at a loss, and stand aimlessly about, facing in all directions. The weather also affects the farmers of the South in a similar manner. Enervated by the summer heat, they cannot muster a sufficient amount of vitality to pull the weeds from their cotton and demand the rights of free-born American citizens at the same time. They become easy prey for the tenant bosses, the land-sharks, and the money-lenders. The July sun, in other words, has been exerting an influence for generations in determining social and economic classes in the South. One's social status can be loosely measured in terms of the inverse ratio of the number of hours spent at the mercy of the July sun.

4

It remains true, however, that the same southern weather which tends to stratify the population also draws the classes together again in a cohesion of interests in the fortunes of King Cotton. This consuming passion, together with a lamentable common interest in King Cawn (which probably did not decrease with prohibition), is strong enough as a force in southern solidarity to offset whatever influences the lack of snow may exert in direct opposition. Especially since the promulgation of President Roosevelt's new deal, the South has come to recognize more and more its community of interest in the fortunes of cotton as a world commodity. Not even the bearing of General Johnson's industrial codes upon the South, particularly with respect to the wage differentials, has given southerners as much of a feeling of regional consciousness as have the various federal programs relating to cotton.

The climate of the South also has an effect upon the nervous systems of the inhabitants. They like pepper in their food, strong coffee, and the excitement of fights.

These tastes are reflected at the dinner table, at lynching bees, and in political campaigns. The southerner, his nerves irritated by the heat, is far more interested in elections than in government; far more concerned over the sporadic eruptions of Red propaganda than over racial or social questions in their broader aspects. At first glance, the transitory and shifting nature of immediate interests in the South appears to be at variance with the region's reputation for traditionalism. But this conflict is only on the surface. Fundamentally the shifting of southern interests—within certain well defined orbits—is in itself one of the most solidly established traditions. In Alabama there is a statue inscribed to "The Man Who Killed Old Abe Lincoln in 1865," and another dedicated to the Boll Weevil in celebration of its contribution to raising the price of cotton by reducing the yield in 1927.

Passing note must also be made of the effect of indigenous diseases in building up a coherent structure of shared experiences in the South. Although malaria is sometimes classified by the natives as being like hookworm and pellagra in implying an unacceptable social status, most southerners in moments of close confidence will admit that they at some time or another have had a touch of malaria, or that they have friends who have had malaria, or at least that they know what a mosquito is like. These experiences, especially when they are treated confidentially, have a way of drawing the people of a region together in a most effective manner. In fact, it might be argued (though not by me) that malaria in the South is almost as potent a factor in the regional solidarity as is the universally shared indignation against the Yankee.

Yet, in final analysis, excellent as are the reasons for southern languor, pleasant as are the relaxations offered by the fields and the streams to the southern mind—sublime as it may be for one to go fishing and invite his soul to search for the secret of the gods in dreamy contemplation—there is much work that ought to be done below the Potomac. The consciences of the southern Bourbons, however, have never held work to be a solemn duty, so far as they themselves have been concerned. Southerners of a less elevated class do labor, of course; they labor hard and long, and, even during the era of the National Recovery Administration, perhaps for fewer cents per unit of energy than do most persons elsewhere in the United States. Nor can one overlook the assiduous application of other southerners, many of whom do not fare so badly in securing adequate returns for their efforts. Among these are the promoters (for their own profit) of such slogans as "Unlimited Natural Resources" and "Cheap Anglo-Saxon Labor." The activities of these gentry—even now, as well as in the 1920's and before that decade—are sufficient, it must be admitted, to threaten the validity of all that I have ever said with reference to southern languor.

But the patterns of the plantation days of long ago still survive in the habits of the privileged classes. Even the operators of gasoline filling stations invariably have black assistants to turn cranks, inflate tires, fill radiators, polish windshields, and perform all the other duties of the establishment—except that of accepting the customers' money. As of old, the climate and the presence of the Negro are the main conditioning elements in southern culture.

Chapter II

Shadows of the Plantation

I

In addition to the amazing influence of the South's pervading sense of class distinctions—which exist in a complicated structure all the way from the lofty Bourbons to the lowly "poor whites" and poor blacks—economic considerations are also effective in the concerted will to keep the weak members of society in an eternal state of subjection. By observing some of the abuses growing out of mortgage and foreclosure proceedings, one may catch a glimpse of the vicious system which frequently is based upon the inability of defenseless sharecroppers and industrial workers to obtain adequate protection from the laws.

Brutal loan-sharks in almost every part of the South thrive upon the Negro's willingness to borrow small sums of money at indefinite rates of interest. On many occasions members of various state legislatures have made determined efforts to pass laws curbing these outrages, but the lobbies of the small-loan operators often have proved too powerful. Affidavits gathered in some investigative studies conducted by a liberal newspaper editor show that as much as 400 per cent of their original loans has been paid by Negroes in a single year. Typical

One sometimes hears the maxim that the letting of Negro shacks is the only real-estate venture sure to bring profit in certain parts of the South.

The Negro has had almost as much as the sunshine to do with conditioning the lives of the white people of the region.

of these affidavits is one signed by a Presbyterian minister
who declared that $115 was paid by the janitor of his
church on a loan of $30 of one year's standing.

Quite generally the operators, of which there may be
as many as fifteen in separate establishments in towns of
about 30,000 population, refuse to allow the Negro
debtors to make payments on the principal sums of their
loans. "You are such a good nigger, Bob," they cajole
the helpless black man, "that I'm going to let you keep
the principal as long as you want it. Just pay me $5 or
$10 as interest whenever you can." By methods of in-
timidation consisting of savage beatings, gestures with
a gun, and threats of jail sentences, the loan-sharks have
been able to keep the more gullible Negroes completely
at their mercy. Almost at will, the lenders are able to
seize the collateral named in promissory notes.

Since the items furnished as security for petty loans
are frequently worth ten times as much as the Negro
borrows, the routine of foreclosure and seizure can be
developed into a profitable business, so long as law en-
forcement does not interfere. For example, the following
items are listed as collateral on a note for two dollars
signed by a Negro in a southern town on April 6, 1929:
". . . the entire crop of corn, cotton, cotton seed and
produce raised or caused to be raised by myself or family
during the year 1929 . . . also 1 perfection #7 oil burning cooking stove has 4 burners, 1 oak finish polar King

refrigerator #25 Ice capacity, 1 oak dresser has 3 drawers & 1 mirror, 1 Black Iron Beadstead . . . has 1 Roll edge cotton mattress and 1 pair of non-folding wire Springs, 4 Cane Seat Straight chairs, 1 oak Rocker with upholstered Seat, 1 9x12 ft art Square colors Green & Red . . . ." Above the scrawled signature of the borrower of two dollars appears the legend, "It is agreed that the property herein mentioned stand as mortgaged security for any amount now due or to become due."

The investigation, which accumulated a number of similar exhibits and many examples of jungle brutality in the collection of debts from Negroes, was undertaken, so I was told, at the request of a branch of the junior chamber of commerce. It seems that, in addition to the general indignation felt in some disinterested quarters, the discomfort of the second-hand furniture dealers had been the main factor in precipitating the attempts at reform. The loan-sharks had begun to monopolize control over the Negro money. Deeply chagrined, and in a fever of self-righteous alarm, the second-hand furniture dealers took the position that they had been on the ground first and that, as a consequence of their being native sons, they were due some prior rights on foreclosures. Their established schedule of selling house furnishings to the Negroes, collecting what they could, and then "pulling" the property, for quick resale to another Negro family, was suffering from unfair competition. Sometimes the small-loan operators, in fact, "pulled" furniture which was the rightful property of the established dealers. Therefore the alert junior chamber of commerce sought to correct these embarrassing complications in the local trade.

2

Interesting variations of such wolf-like practices are described in *The Store*, a book for which Mr. T. S. Stribling was awarded the Pulitzer prize for fiction in 1933. Readers of this justly severe arraignment of a despicable economic system should carefully bear in mind that the main protagonist of the novel, Colonel Vaiden, is a former plantation overseer, and therefore a member of a shabby and degraded class, which is not to be confused with the genuine southern squirearchy. My own reaction to *The Store* is that while the book is impressively loaded with artistic and factual truth, it shares with *Elmer Gantry* the fault of being misleading as a social study, for the reason that it portrays chicaneries which would be typical if distributed among a number of individuals, but which are not typical when concentrated *in toto* as characteristics of a single individual. I should not, however, attempt to dispose of the book as did a person who inquired of the book-review editor of a southern publication "whether the fact that Oscar DePriest is said to have been born on a plantation near

Florence [Alabama] had anything to do with Mr. Stribling's choice of scene," or as did another disturbed reader
who connected "Mr. Stribling's ancestry (by implica-
tion) with the invading outlaws from Tennessee who
committed all kinds of depredations, and consistently
voted the Republican ticket."

It is not to be understood that Negroes alone are the
victims of these vicious systems of petty exploitation.
Powerless white people suffer too. During the present
difficult times, as a matter of fact, Negroes frequently
are given preference in employment as sharecroppers.
This racial favoritism, however, is not sentimental. The
Negroes are said to work for less and to be easier to manage than the whites of the tenant-farmer class.

In their dealings, real-estate tricksters also appear to
exhibit a preference for the black people. One sometimes
hears the maxim that the letting of Negro shacks is the
only real-estate venture sure to bring a profit in certain
parts of the South. Usually constructed along back alleys
or railroad tracks, the two-room huts can be erected for
$85 or $90; those with five rooms might cost $200 or
$225. They can be rented steadily for $1.25 or $2.50 a
week, and they never demand any repairs. Now and then
a really knowing person can extend his holdings of
Negro shacks with an even smaller original outlay. He
can suggest to a Negro happening to own a house the
desirability of treating the property to the unusual luxury

of a good painting. If the black proprietor is short of funds, the sharp dealer himself might advance the money needed for the refurbishing, take a mortgage on the whole property, and in due time foreclose. The many sleight-of-hand performances of this nature are not entirely confined to white practitioners. Some of the most dastardly economic crimes are committed against the Negroes by treacherous members of their own race.

3

My contention is not that the jealous hatred of the so-called poor whites and the petty economic exploitations are wholly responsible for whatever injustices may hang upon the shoulders of the black man today. Below the surface of these major factors, there is an important historical root which explains a tendency of reputable southern people of the older generation to look with horror upon suggestions that the franchise and jury service might ever be freely extended to the Negro in the South. These older people still remember "the tragic era," when the vengeance of Stevens and Sumner lay heavily upon the South. They vividly recall the efforts of the original Ku Klux Klan and the Order of the White Camellia to preserve the white South against the domination of Negroes who were in the power of scalawags and carpet-baggers.

Men now fifty years old will tell you how their

fathers in tidewater Virginia, fifty years ago, would place high-powered rifles conspicuously in the rear of their buggies on election days in districts where the Negroes outnumbered the whites ten to one. The rifles, with their magnifying-glass sights, would never be removed from the buggies. No disorder took place. The white planters would simply gather quietly in small groups and remain near the voting places, often the grange houses, from early morning until sundown. The Negroes would be there too, chatting pleasantly enough among themselves and with the white men; but the steel muzzles peeping from the rear of the buggies always served to send home their messages of discretion.

In those days in Virginia the Republican ballots were printed on rather coarse brown paper, while names of the Democratic candidates appeared on "lily white" paper of a smooth texture. When it was found that voting boxes obviously had been stuffed, the settled procedure was for a respected citizen to stand blindfolded and draw from the box a number of ballots sufficient to make the remaining total correspond to the number of qualified voters in the community. On one occasion the Sunday school superintendent was chosen for this duty. For several days before the drawing he could be seen going about with his fingers busily engaged in the side-pockets of his coat. Actually, he was training his finger-tips to be sensitive to the difference between the coarse texture of the Repub-

lican ballot and the smooth finish of the "lily white"
paper. On the day of the scheduled drawing, this man
of religion, though heavily blindfolded like Justice herself, was able to extract only Republican ballots from
the box, and the election was officially a triumph for the
Democrats. A story is told of the corresponding period
in Selma, Alabama, where the Democrats persuaded a
circus manager to accept Republican poll-tax receipts as
tickets to the show. The Negro voters were encouraged
to attend the circus, and the Democrats won the election.

These instances illustrate the devices employed by the
"best people" of the South half a century ago. What
they did to keep the Negro from voting was illegal of
course; but, being themselves officially deprived of the
ballot by reason of the Civil War amendments, their
practical nullification of the fourteenth amendment was
then necessary for their own self-preservation.

But the contemporary picture is vastly different. The
"best people" of the South, have gone far toward regain-
ing their feet. Certainly they no longer find it necessary
to employ devious means in protecting their own welfare
against any racial menace. The more reputable southern
people also have recovered to a large extent from the
terrific onslaughts begun against them by the Populists
in the 1890's. The recent hullabaloo over "white supremacy" has been a cheap and degraded imitation of the
efforts of superior white people of past generations to

avoid annihilation. Similarly, the recent revivals of the Ku Klux Klan have represented the spurious endeavors of the lower middle class to imitate the defensive measures identified with the genteel Order of the White Camellia of bygone days, and with the picturesque Ku Klux Klan during the short interval when it was led by General Forrest and sanctioned by General Lee before abuses of its honorable regalia resulted in its disbandment in 1869.

4

In view of the well established background of class discrimination on economic lines, it is not in the least surprising that shadows of the southern plantation should have extended into the new industrial system which swept over parts of the South during the boom preceding the depression. Sudden migration of machinery from the North furnished a number of opportunities for the idea of agricultural peonage to spread over the mushroom factory towns. In numerous instances, former sharecroppers became mill hands.

Mindful of the terrible shadows remaining from the labor tragedies of 1930, two years ago, in the early summer of 1932, we drove our automobile through the quiet streets of Gastonia. A four-lane highway of gleaming white pavement had borne us swiftly over the twelve miles from Charlotte. I had been addressing a postal card to a friend whom I wished to inform with all dispatch that we had just seen the new *two-million-dollar* chapel at Duke University, which seemed in some inexplicable way to be connected with the splendid highway which we were traversing and with the great mills which we were soon to reach.

The roadway had been so smooth that I had been able to hold the postal card on my lap and write without the least jostling of the fountain pen. Huge letters on the inner lanes frequently warned

ONLY

PASSING

FOR

in that strange new language, so appropriately designed for the machine age, which is to be read upside down. We accepted the adjuration against defiance of the laws of nature. Thoughtful highway engineers wished to avoid a collision between momentous forces moving in opposite directions. What more serious calamities might have been avoided if a particle of such foresight had been applied to the larger and more inclusive projects in social engineering which had gone forward in that vicinity! What desolation from the impact of crossed human purposes might have been prevented!

Quite unwilling to pass through Gastonia with only a glimpse at the brick sides of the bulking factories inter-

nationally famed for the stretch-out system, and not especially caring to visit them, we compromised by drawing
up at a little gasoline and sandwich station of rough unpainted boards on the farther outskirts of the town. The
foothills of smoky blue mountains ranged off on our right.
We might have reached them in half an hour's walk
through the green June fields. As we halted in front of
the "shoppe," it seemed judicious that we have a brace
of hamburger sandwiches and two bottles of pop.

Our host was in a slough of despond concerning his
business. He had once gone from North Carolina to
Washington, where he had worked as a clerk until the
longing for Carolina hills had drawn him home. Now
determined to return to Washington, he was of half a
mind to take up with the bonus marchers of the American Legion, who were coming by his door in a few
days. He apologized for having no barbecue sauce for
the hamburgers. Our assurance that this omission troubled us not at all appeared to invite an understanding
spirit between us as we sat there in the hot sun, with the
glorious mountains in view.

"Nobody here is making anything," he said. The great
new mill which had caused most of the trouble carried
over a hundred thousand spindles. It was one of the largest
in the South. Under normal conditions it would give
employment to more than 2,000 operatives. Some years
ago the workers had been recruited by labor agents paid

$6.00 and $8.00 a day to travel through the hills of the Carolinas, Georgia, and Tennessee. The natives forsook their cabins in the mountains for Gastonia on the promise of $10 a week in the mills. "You ought to see some of those folks from the mountains. They don't know nothing—just enough to get up and follow the path to the mill and then to take the path to their house again when the whistle blows."

Concentration of the cotton industry in Gastonia resulted in the location there of some fifty mills. In the county as a whole there were about a hundred mills. Stringent competition had forced a gradual reduction of wages from $18 to $11 a week in the case of the more highly paid employes. A head mechanic in a town near by, who was a friend of our host, had suffered a decrease in wages from $41 to $19 a week. Then came the celebrated stretch-out system, by means of which many operatives were laid off and the remaining workers forced to tend an additional number of spindles. That was the *casus belli* of the Communist revolt. The strike was fearful. All the mill workers were bewildered. They didn't know what it was all about. "That woman was killed just at the bend of the road about two hundred yards down there. See that post with the Anti-Nox sign on it? That's where it happened."

Everything in Gastonia dated from the strike. Before the strike apartments in town rented for $60; now "they beg you to take them for $12." The mill workers were able to put in an average of only one and a half days a week on the job. All the company managements were doing the best they could. They would send families back to the farm and give them fertilizer for a crop. Vegetable gardening was encouraged. "It costs them less to do those things than to keep the people in food at the company houses," explained our cynical host. "Some big shots in the state must have gone down to Raleigh and made the companies do something about the idle hands around here. I don't know how it happened."

Taking our pop bottles after we had finished drinking, he said that eight years previously he had come up to Gastonia from a farm near Shelby to run a store for the mill workers. He had thought there was a rainbow over the factory town. At first it was wonderful. Everybody was making plenty of money. Now he had been too long away from the farm to go back. Seeing the world only in the light of his own predicament, he left us with a dejected shrug. "There's nothing left for anybody in North Carolina," he said. "Maybe things will improve when we get Hoover out of the White House." Caught by the words of some bush-shelling political demagogue of the depression, the transplanted hill youth from the environs of Shelby feebly sought another rainbow. Over parts of North Carolina politicians attempting to capitalize upon the depression had placed signs reading "You

Can't Eat Paved Roads." Perhaps he had seen one of those. The influence of a predatory industrial expansion had left its mark upon this specimen of "cheap Anglo-Saxon labor." Mayhap, however, he should be classed among the "unlimited natural resources," of which the Gastonia industrialists used to boast before the strikes and before the depression.

As a matter of fact, the bitterness professed by what was left of Gastonia's working population in the early summer of 1932 did not seem to be aimed directly at any clearly recognized enemy. Rather it was a diffused and divagating sense of frustration. As they sat barefooted on their front porches in the warm sunshine, toying with small hickory twigs at the snuff planted between cheek and gum, what they seemed to feel was an inept and inchoate numbness of mind and body. To all appearances, they were of all God's creatures the lost, the forlorn, the unshepherded.

On their side, the mill owners were not entirely to blame for the catastrophes which took place at Gastonia. Neither are the Communists nor the chamber of commerce propagandists to be named as wholly responsible. Under the circumstances, all concerned were doing what they could to meet an unhappy turn of fortune. Gastonia, Elizabethton, and Marion should be memorable as three of the more tragic by-products of the meeting of the industrial revolution with relics of the plantation system in the southern part of the United States. Thomas Carlyle and John Ruskin, if they were alive, would be much interested in the recent histories of these three towns.

Down the highway from Gastonia towards Spartanburg, South Carolina, we saw a rickety truck overloaded with cotton bales on the way to the mills. The load careened far over on one side. As we watched it move up the road behind us, we expected it to fall into the ditch every time it swayed on the wrenched body of the truck. A little farther along the magnificent highway, six or eight ragged children were eating green plums, their bare feet clutching the loose soil of a red-clay embankment. At the entrance to the next town a large sign proclaimed: "Watch Gaffney Grow!"

5

Lengthening shadows from the plantation era, together with a labor leadership which has often lacked a basic understanding of southern characteristics, have militated against the success of organized movements among the working populations of the South. First, there has been the survival of the caste system, which rests upon the assumption that class distinctions should be rigidly maintained; and second, the organization of unions has been difficult in branches of industry in which whites and Negroes are engaged in the same type of work. That occupational class consciousness now and then overlaps racial lines, however, has been demonstrated in some of the recent coal strikes, when white and Negro miners have been observed marching together in support of their common objectives. But the outcome of the 1934 general textile strike clearly indicated that a uniformity of feeling is anything but marked among the working classes of the South.

If barriers erected by traditional and racial considerations have retarded organization by industrial workmen, these bulwarks against change have been far more noticeable in connection with the utterly futile efforts of agricultural workers to form sharecroppers' unions. With respect to sharecroppers' unions, especially where Negroes have been concerned, the southern conscience has been content to treat them as manifestations growing out of Red propaganda, and the sheriffs, as a rule, have dealt with such cases in short order. The under-privileged white man has his choice of staying on the land and trusting to the erratic beneficence of an absentee landlord for his "rations" and overalls, or of going off with his family to one of the factories situated in the nearest town. In such a dilemma, many tenant farmers, in spite of their poverty and hopelessness, would agree with Jeeter Lester in Erskine Caldwell's *Tobacco Road.* "The Lord made the land," said Jeeter, "and He put me here to raise crops on it. I been doing that, and my daddy before me, for the past fifty years, and that's what's intended. Them

durn cotton mills is for the women folks to work in.
They ain't no place for a man to be, fooling away with
little wheels and strings all day long. I say, it's a hell of a
job for a man to spend his time winding strings on
spools."

But the disreputable old Jeeter does not have much to
look forward to on the land either. Customarily the
southern tenant farmer, white or black, has an average
monthly income of some $10 in money. No doubt that
is why $7.50 or $10 a week in the new cotton mills seems
like great wealth to him; he does not realize that living
costs are higher in the mill towns. In March the typical
tenant borrows about $200 from his landlord or banker.
Of this sum, $50 may be designated for the fertilizer
dealer, another $50 for the stock-feed merchant, and $10
reserved for interest. In September or October, with
luck, he may sell three bales of cotton for $200—although
prices during the past several years have not brought him
anything like that much. Then the farmer pays off his
loan, and has left about $15 for each of the six months
until the next March, when the yearly cycle starts again.
During the year he may have a few chickens, raise some
scrubby vegetables, or sell a few loads of stove wood to
eke out his meager living. Under misfortune he may not
be able to meet his note in the autumn; whereupon he
falls neatly into the hands of the absentee landlord, for
better or worse. Since warehouse receipts and ginning

One's social status can be loosely measured in terms of the inverse ratio of the number of hours spent at the mercy of the July sun.

During the year the tenant farmer may have a few chickens, raise some scrubby vegetables, or sell a few loads of stove wood. He may not be able to meet his note in the autumn, whereupon he falls neatly into the hands of the absentee landlord, for better or worse.

reports enable the landlords to check up easily on the tenant's honesty in reporting the amount of his cotton crop, landowners and bankers have often discouraged rotation and diversification by exacting prohibitively large shares of other crops which are difficult to check.

Although various programs of the federal government undoubtedly have been influential in raising the prices of cotton in the South, there is some question as to whether they have been of any appreciable assistance to the tenant farmer. Evidence introduced at federal court trials in the South in 1933 showed that many of the seed-loan checks made out to hundreds of tenant farmers had found their way pretty directly to the hands of money-lenders and merchants in country towns where a practice is made of "advancing" such things as fat meat, sugar, snuff, fertilizer, stick candy, denim, calico, kerosene, chill tonics, kidney pills, and a few dollars to these lean and uncouth mortals who somehow manage to carry the burdens of southern slavery in these modern times.

Just now it is too early to attempt to estimate the value of the crop-reduction programs, including the Bankhead bill, which have been undertaken by the Agricultural Adjustment Administration in the South. It is well known that the intensive cultivation of reduced acreages, coupled with excellent growing conditions, produced more cotton in 1933 than was made in 1932, in spite of the "plow-under" campaign of the AAA. Senator Bankhead was entirely correct in his position that the amount of cotton ginned, rather than the number of acres planted, would have to be relied upon by the government as a basis of measurement in any practicable plan to control the production. Perhaps an effective solution to the South's problem of over-production of cotton may yet be found through the instrumentality of federal supervision. But it seems fair to say that as yet the tenant farmer's plight has not been given the attention it deserves in the government's approach to the problem.

Peter Molyneaux, who edits the *Texas Weekly* at Dallas, stands in the forefront of a group of southerners which has consistently opposed the crop-reduction theory on the ground that the government could aid the southern farmer best by opening foreign trade channels to cotton from the South. Mr. Molyneaux implies that, while we have carried the tenant system forward from plantation days, the tariff policy of the United States has resulted in a "nationalism" which has made it impossible for the South to continue to enjoy the benefits of large-scale cotton exportation, which also was an essential characteristic of the plantation economy. In a pamphlet entitled *What Economic Nationalism Means to the South* (published jointly by the Foreign Policy Association and the World Peace Foundation), Mr. Molyneaux calls attention to the fact that 81 per cent of all the cotton produced in the South prior to the Civil War was exported, and that "cotton constituted more than 57 per cent of the total exports of the United States in 1860." Although the world has come to depend upon the South for more than 40 per cent of its cotton supply, there is at present a grave danger—if I correctly interpret the views of the Texas editor—that the combination of the government's tariff policy and its crop-reduction program invites such nations as Egypt, India, and Russia to deprive the South of a large share of its income from its exportations. But these, after all, are matters for the experts.

Rupert Vance's *Human Geography of the South* offers the following picture of how the plantation system of the Old South gave way to the tenant method of agriculture: "A stricken upper class possessing nothing but lands met a servile population possessed of naught except the labor of their hands. In what must have been an era of primitive barter, a system was arrived at whereby labor was secured without money wages and land without money rent. Up and down the Cotton Belt southern states after 1865 vied with one another in passing crop lien laws. Accepted as the temporary salvation of a wrecked economic structure, the system has increasingly set the mode for southern agriculture. . . . The most outstanding commentary one can make on the South is to point out the fact that from that day to this the percentage of those who must secure this year's livelihood by crop liens has steadily increased." Mr. Vance then proceeds to show that between

1920 and 1930 the percentage of tenancy in ten chief cotton states increased from 55 to 61.5.

While it is obviously impossible to gauge exactly the effect of the government's crop-reduction program upon unemployment among persons of the tenant-farmer class, the rolls of the Federal Emergency Relief Administration in some parts of the South have been crowded with the names of sharecroppers no longer needed by landlords who had signed agreements to raise less cotton. Furthermore, in its program of rural rehabilitation in the South, the FERA was baffled by not a few cases in which landlords at the same time refused to advance money to their cash renters and also refused to waive the rent of these tenants in order to allow them the benefits of direct federal relief. These landlords apparently preferred to hold the remnants of the old plantation system in their own hands; they did not relish "outside interference."

Thus it may be seen that the case of Erskine Caldwell's Jeeter Lester is not a rare one these days in the South. In spite of his tattered degradation and his wretched obscenity, there remains in Jeeter's mind one shred of beauty—a beauty which the South ought to consider worth preserving. "Captain John told the merchants in Fuller not to let me have no more snuff and rations on his credit," says Jeeter to his son-in-law, "and I don't know where to get nothing. I'd raise a crop of my own on this land if I could get somebody to sign my guano-notes, but won't nobody do that for me, neither. That's what I'm wanting to do powerful strong right now. When the winter goes, and when it gets to be time to burn off broom-sedge in the fields and underbrush in the thickets, I sort of want to cry, I reckon it is. The smell of that sedge-smoke this time of the year near about drives me crazy. Then pretty soon all the other farmers start plowing. That's what gets under my skin the worst. When the smell of that new earth turning over behind the plows strikes me, I get all weak and shaky. It's in my blood—burning broom-sedge and plowing in the ground this time of year. . . . Us Lesters sure like to stir the earth and make plants grow in it. . . . The land has got a powerful hold on me."

What, if one may inquire, is the attitude of the southern conscience with reference to Jeeter's wanting to make a crop? Or, in case he gives up and moves away to a cotton mill village, what has the regional sense of right and wrong to say about what happens to him there?

Chapter III

Garlands of Straw

I

To those gallant southerners who doubt not that the twentieth century is a loathsome span between Appomattox and the New Jerusalem, conscience must imply only the melancholy duty of trimming candles in front of images of the South before the War Between the States. The suggestion that problems below the Potomac might enlist their sense of moral responsibility would impress them as a double-jointed heresy.

Among the southerners, however, there are some fallen angels who occasionally are tempted to wonder whether the South has any conscience at all. Forced to contemplate the tenant-farming system, the low industrial wage scales, hookworm and malaria, and moonshine whiskey in their region, these skeptical ones sometimes go so far as to suspect that the southern conscience, if it ever existed, probably was among the other Confederate virtues which died at Appomattox. While these individuals revere the Old South for the beauty and the charm which it undoubtedly once possessed in certain areas, they find that they cannot always escape a disagreeable present by relying upon mental flights into the past.

I have been told on good authority of a town in the

far South where a group of old men still live in their very dear memories of another time. They have two major pretenses: they drink moonshine whiskey, which they call julep; and they play poker quite formally for stakes running into hundreds of dollars, although they have no money. At the end of each game they solemnly clink goblets, propose toasts to the winners, and present their I.O.U.'s. The papers are precisely folded and placed in waistcoat pockets, whereupon the rather splendid old beggars go home and tear them up. Such a tale, illustrating in an exaggerated form an attitude which is widespread in parts of the South, may quaintly attest the wistful feeling for the olden times. It may also be a token of decadence. At any rate, it bears no warrant for the future.

On Sunday afternoons in spring, motorists are inclined to pause in little southern towns, such as those in which these old men would be at home, to see the roses and japonicas. The roses are mostly of the cream-colored variety which climbs richly over brick walls. They are cool, luxurious and restful like pearls and white satin. But the red japonicas are riotous and thrilling. There is nothing serene about them. Shining in the broad yards of old dwellings, their vitality each year is an emblem of reassurance. Through the winters they remain constant; in the spring they bloom.

Behind the japonicas, the houses are not pretentious,

but they are rightly designed. Whoever built them possessed restraint and dignity of soul, and enough skill to express these qualities in form and line. As for the populations, they give the impression of being made up only of the very old and the very young, as if the towns were peopled entirely by children on visits to their grandparents. Here one can understand the background of Stark Young's *So Red the Rose*, and one can feel the meaning of Mr. Young's observation, which appeared in an essay a few years ago, that his conception of aristocracy hinged upon the memory of his uncle sitting quietly talking on the front porch throughout long summer evenings "one after another." In everything one senses the lack of the contemporaneous. Nor is the reason for this lack difficult to ascertain. For at least two generations many of the promising youths of the towns, after their graduation from high school, have sought careers for themselves in distant cities; and girls of the same age and of similar promise have gone away to colleges or boarding schools, later to find husbands who take them to live far from the cream-colored roses and the red japonicas of their childhood. Neither the girls nor the boys have been able to envision a satisfactory future for themselves at home.

Even today there are a few—a very few—anachronistic manorial estates which, in a sense, may be said to preserve

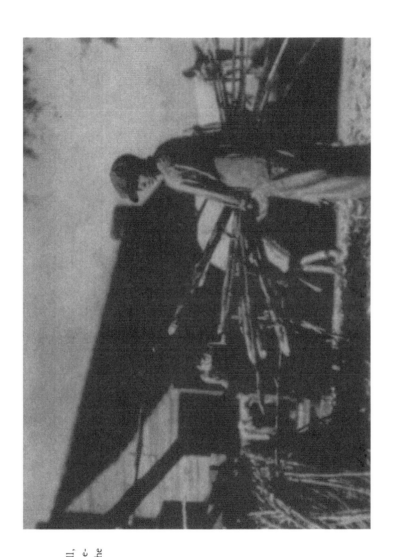

Like the old-fashioned grist mill, this sorghum mill lies midway between the industrial age and the agricultural era.

A Slovakian digging pottery clay in Alabama.

the vitality which they possessed before the Civil War. Still living in the light of other years along the loamy banks of the Mississippi River's last two hundred miles, a plantation master today rides leisurely over a portion of his three thousand acres during the middle hours of the morning. At noon he returns to his ancestral mansion, discards his riding attire, enjoys a calm and restful bath, and presents himself at the family board for a long and heavy dinner. He will wish to lean back in his chair for a conversation between courses. The repast may consume as much as two hours, not counting the coffee which may follow on the verandah. After such a dinner he is, from force of custom and physical necessity, through for the day. Consequently, the afternoon is really evening in effect—a fact which possibly offers one explanation of the peculiar meaning of the word "evening" in the southern part of the United States.

But this plantation master, charming as his complacent existence may be—what was he doing while his fellow Mississippians were electing Theodore G. Bilbo to the United States Senate? And his Bourbon friends across the river in Louisiana—what have they done about Huey P. Long? Can it be that the aristocratic conscience no longer feels any responsibility for the dignified government of southern commonwealths?

2

Reliance for illusionary grandeur upon a somewhat legendary past is, of course, in part the natural result of a sense of frustration and temporary impotence. Nevertheless, the persistence of this supine philosophy over the seven decades since the Civil War would seem to indicate a more serious weakness. Charles A. Beard and other historians have attempted to puncture the theory that there was a marked difference between the colonial settlers of the South and those of the New England states. And there seems to be little reason to assume that English aristocrats, and near-aristocrats, along the Atlantic seaboard lost their gentle blood by crossing the Appalachian Mountains north of the Potomac River instead of south of that stream. But that they unquestionably did so is a popular conviction in the southern states. People of Memphis and Vicksburg find it hard indeed to understand how the Father of Waters could ever have selected a channel which lay through Minneapolis and St. Paul.

That the pioneers, after moving westward from the Atlantic coast, found the cultural environment different in the South from what it was in the North goes without saying. But there is at least room for debate over whether geography, rather than blood inheritance, was not the principal factor in determining differences between the northerner and the southerner as we recognize the two

types at the present time. Again, that the native southerner, if he has had a happy life, should appreciate and
love his own region above all others is natural. But the
tendencies of people of the South to insist vociferously
upon all occasions that everything southern, from various
kinds of biscuits to the beauties of womanhood, is superior to everything northern are dangerously suggestive
of what the psychologists used to call an inferiority complex, or an over-compensation for a subconsciously-
recognized weakness. For southerners to cleave to the
idea that anything alien, from safety matches to social
reforms, must be viewed with suspicion is even worse,
from the point of view of taste alone, if for no other reasons. To me, the blue-grass section of Kentucky, the green
valleys of central Tennessee, the parts of Mississippi and
Alabama which border along the Gulf of Mexico, the
mountains of North Carolina, and the Shenandoah Valley of Virginia have a loveliness unmatched by natural
beauties which I happen to have seen elsewhere in the
United States. But I have heard New England people
speak of the mountains of New Hampshire and Vermont
with a considerable amount of fond emotion. Residents
of Colorado imply that the rest of us are only half alive.
And then there are always California and the Cali-
fornians.

The temptation to confuse geographical influences

with forces due to fundamental differences in human stock is one which southerners must take care to guard themselves against. I confess that I have a particular aversion to the flat prairies of the Middle West. When one rides in an automobile over the unending paved roads of Indiana and Illinois, or through the eternal aisles of cornstalks in Iowa, he is aware of the verdant sheaves and stalks of the plants and of the final conquest of the land to man's support and profit. Yet he may be wearied and oppressed by what seems to him to be the really horrible monotony of the scene. He moves, it may appear to him, for hour after hour without an iota's change in the landscape; he may see no indications of his progress except the signposts on the road. His imagination may be distressed as he moves on and on. He wishes that he might move faster and faster so as to reach the horizon line at once. Perhaps he is not moving at all, though the speedometer registers sixty miles an hour. Even the odors may impress him as being the same: fecund earth, succulent growths, fertilizer and hay; he may welcome the breath from pig wallows, thinking that they furnish at least a break in the monotony. The motorist may feel that he would like to get out and walk, to stride over the limitless fields, so as to provide a change in method of movement to compensate for the unbroken sameness of the view. But there are persons (including Willa Cather, the Virginian who

was transplanted to Nebraska) who consider the prairies
of the Middle West extremely beautiful. And it must be
conceded that not all of that section of the United States
is a flat plain.

At the same time, having felt the disagreeable sensa-
tions which I have just described, I once was led to believe that I could interpret the middle western people in
terms of my own impressions of their prairie lands. It
seemed to me that my personal emotional reactions had
given me the key to the restless urge of the middle western pioneers: the pent-up nervousness of their bodies,
their determination to push their acreages farther and
farther toward the horizon, their relentless and almost
pathological recourse to racking, burdensome toil, their
isolation from the refreshing influence of change. It was
my theory that the social characteristics of the Middle
West were as flat as the plains which the people tilled.
That the people knew only the compelling desire to sub-
due more and more of the land to the uses of the plow
and the sickle was my analysis of the culture of the corn
and wheat country. As the mariner on the sea—so I rea-
soned with perhaps some injustice to such characters as
those portrayed by Joseph Conrad and John Masefield—
has but one ultimate pattern, which he constantly repeats
from voyage to voyage, that of working with all his
strength to pass beyond the monotony of the waves, so

the prairie dweller of the Middle West toiled single-mindedly at his plow, work being his only recourse, his only means of accomplishment.

But last summer I spent some days in an Illinois town which had just been depicted, in Janet Ayer Fairbank's novel called *The Bright Land,* as having been the scene of a romance quite as flattering to the community as anything which has come from the pens of southern fiction writers with special attachments to the early years in their own part of the United States. The New England heroine of this novel, arriving with her husband at their new home and still under the influence of the distasteful impressions she had received during their long stagecoach ride over the prairies, had cried with relief: "Oh, Stephen—*trees!* And actually—*hills!*" This land—which had caused the girl from New England to exclaim, "So bright! Such an immense sky, much bigger than ours in New England!"—had been settled mainly by people who had made their way up the Mississippi River from New Orleans and St. Louis in the days when what is now Chicago was an Indian trading post on the swampy shores of Lake Michigan. With them on the river boats they had brought mahogany furniture, their carriages, draperies, laces, silverware, and sometimes their African slaves. Later they were joined by settlers who had traveled overland from Virginia and Massachusetts. They had terraced the steep hillsides by erecting high stone walls to hold the earth in place, and the red and gray slate of the mansard roofs of their three-story brick houses caught the sun above the thick foliage of lofty elms and oaks. At the foot of one of their sloping streets, they had built an Episcopal church of heavy stone blocks, inside of which the later arrivals had been able to admire carved wood and brass fixtures, stained glass windows and a small pipe organ which had been brought over from England by way of New Orleans and the Mississippi River.

Motivated perhaps by their belief that the African retainers were unhappy during the long and cold winter season, or perhaps by the realization that the Negroes were not particularly useful in the wheat and corn fields, in the lead mines or in the trapping of fur-bearing animals—or possibly by a subtle influence of the New England conscience—the early inhabitants of "the bright land" soon either freed their slaves or shipped them southward down the river. The fact that, some years later, these people for a time concentrated upon the making of lead bullets for the soldiers of Abraham Lincoln during the Civil War—while it well might induce gallant southerners to regard them as villains of the deepest dye—can never wholly erase their claim to a rather eminent social respectability.

It may be that I am a little biased in favor of "the bright land" in view of the entirely personal reason that

I happen to have been married in the stone church to which reference has been made. But I am inclined to believe that other southerners can show even less justification for their blind prejudices which so often lead them to assume that the South at one time enjoyed the only really elevated civilization that the United States has ever known. Even the Middle West has its traditions.

3

I should be the last to deny the possibility of making an impressive case for the aristocratic, or squirearchal, culture that existed in some parts of the South before the Civil War. But I cannot feel that the most vocal present-day champions of the Old South have proved very convincing. The Nashville agrarians undoubtedly have much powerful evidence on their side, but have they not tended to exercise more emotion than cerebration as to the material that they have introduced into their arguments? (Although we noticed on the outskirts of Nashville a year or so ago a radio broadcasting station which boasted of having the tallest tower of the kind in the country, we failed to ascertain whether the agrarians were speaking over it.) Apparently the members of the Nashville group have set out to protect what they define as the southern way of life against perilous influences, which they believe to be embodied in industrialism and liberalism. While the agrarians individually possess creative talents that demand

In final analysis, excellent as are the reasons for southern languor, pleasant as are the relaxations offered by the fields and the streams to the southern mind, sublime as it may be for one to go fishing . . . there is much work that ought to be done below the Potomac.

A "boxed" house with a "board" roof, of a type common in the Tennessee valley.

respect, there is some question as to whether they in every case have improved their personal reputations by undertaking to stand collectively for a credo that takes no account of contemporary social evils so often traceable, in the opinion of other southerners, to the very way of life which the agrarians attempt to uphold. If, as Gerald W. Johnson once hinted, the Tennessee traditionalists do not consider the ravages of the loan-sharks, the unfairness of the tenant-farming system, and the Negro problem worthy of serious consideration at the present time, thereby exhibiting a willingness to ignore significant conditions which lie under their noses, how can they be trusted to maintain a clear-sighted perspective with reference to a ramified social structure that existed almost a century ago?

Finally, one might naturally expect that the agrarians, if recognized as the authentic voices of southern traditionalism, would have received their most active support from South Carolina and Virginia, as well as from elderly gentlemen who once were associated with the dominant class of the Old South. Yet, such South Carolinians and Virginians as Julia Peterkin, DuBose Heyward, Josephine Pinckney, Ellen Glasgow, Virginius Dabney, and James Branch Cabell do not see eye to eye with the Nashville group. And when the agrarians issued *I'll Take My Stand* in 1930, John Crowe Ransom not only was challenged to a debate in New Orleans by W. S. Knickerbocker, the Yankee professor of English at Sewanee, Tennessee, but also was attacked, with at least a certain amount of sarcasm, by Stringfellow Barr, editor of *The Virginia Quarterly Review*, before a large audience in Richmond. Four years later the publication of the symposium entitled *Culture in the South*, which did not blink at contemporary realities, was received with certain reservations by some of the southern magazines and newspapers, but none of them printed with respect to *Culture in the South* the kind of devastating criticism with which in several instances they had met the manifesto of the Tennessee traditionalists. In fact, Jonathan Daniels, associate editor of the Raleigh *News and Observer*, may have been close to the truth when he suggested in *The Saturday Review of Literature* that the agrarians ought to be associated with the Populists, rather than with the aristocrats, since their position depends so much upon a partly jealous antagonism towards the well-to-do industrialists of the New South.

Nor can it be said that the agrarians have succeeded in enlisting the support of all the individuals who at this time represent a link between the ante-bellum South and the South of textile strikes and wage differentials. Before the North Carolina Bar Association during the summer of 1934, Judge Robert W. Winston delivered an address which he called "A Garland for Ashes: an Aspiration for the South." Because of Judge Winston's admission that

he once owned a one-fourth share in three slaves and because he is the author of volumes on Robert E. Lee,
Andrew Johnson, and Jefferson Davis, he should have
the right to his say on matters of regional interest. To
the lawyers he declared: "Lee advised his people to forget
bitterness and become good American citizens. General
Lee is depicted as sad and dejected and at last filling a dis-
consolate grave. . . . He was not that sort; he was the exact
opposite. Having submitted the issues dividing the North
and the South to the sword and lost, Robert E. Lee surrendered, and when he surrendered, he went down to a
peaceful rest, one of the most honored and contented of
men." Judge Winston is not friendly to the thought of
spending the rest of his days shedding idle tears over
Appomattox. "In God's name," he exclaimed in his address, "let us get into the game! or else let us secede
again!"

Such pronouncements as this, together with the realization that it is possible for younger southerners to attempt
to deal with facts without always being pilloried for
heresy, should have a profound meaning for the present
generation in the South. Without irreverence to what
was beautiful in the culture of the Old South, persons living below the Potomac today cannot afford to make a
fetish of the southern plantation before the Civil War.
The plantation, which has been the subject of so much
romantic fiction, was anything but the universal form of

economic and social organization in the ante-bellum South. Ulrich B. Phillips's *Life and Labor in the Old South* tells us that, judging from the census figures for 1860, "the planter class numbered less than a quarter of a million souls in the fifteen commonwealths" on the eve of the Civil War. According to Mr. Phillips, there were "nearly six of the eight million whites out of proprietary touch with the four million slaves."

It is to be expected that those who persist in maintaining a hooded vision of the past should also fail to grasp a full picture of what lies before their very eyes. Downright ignorance of the facts frequently is responsible for this faulty perception. Again, there is the weak tendency to avoid baffling realities of the present by taking refuge in a partly fictitious past. Still left perplexed, however, by the South's inclination to sulk as Achilles did in his tent, disrespectful critics might seek a medical explanation for our failure to get into the game. Such critics might look favorably upon a theory that the long prevalence of malaria in the southern lowlands has contrived to produce a malarial mind in the inhabitants. They might press the argument that the influences of the regional mythology and those of the epidemics of malaria, because of an electric affinity which they have for each other, have been fused in such a way as to pervade the southern mind with a dreamy and miasmic lethargy. It is just as well for southern complacency that science probably could not bear out such a theory on the basis of data that are now available. For one thing, local health officers have been known to suppress figures dealing with malaria on the ground that they "look bad for the community." It may be fantastic to blame the mosquito entirely for the malarial mind wherever it occurs in the South. Yet, the South must take to heart the lesson taught by its own General William Crawford Gorgas in his sanitary work in the Panama Canal Zone before the full human energy of the region can be released into constructive channels.

On the whole, the future of the South cannot be served by that state of mind which holds that any critical examination of our past must be regarded as a sacrilege. True loyalty to the South demands that we boldly grapple with the fact that our historical stereotypes have now and then been smirched with elements of cruelty and sham.

Chapter IV
Pulpit and Pew

I

NOTHING would be gained by contending that the South is the only section of the United States whose record bears dark stains from cruelty and sham. But Georgians and Mississippians cannot wholly justify their tolerance of Judge Lynch through the argument that the rope and faggot have not been unknown in Iowa and Nebraska and that California and Maryland were the scenes of two of the most savage exhibitions of mob violence in recent years. It is not enough for Alabamians, distressed over "outside criticisms" of the Scottsboro case, to call attention to what happened to Sacco and Vanzetti in Massachusetts and to Mooney and Billings in California.

Many examples of strange connections between pseudo-religious professions and barbaric cruelties in other parts of the nation can readily be called to mind. For instance, James Truslow Adams, in his *The Epic of America*, brings up some terrible illustrations of the perversions of the New England conscience by the mill owners who in the 1840's often attempted to express holy reasons for their determination to keep children at work from twelve to fourteen hours a day. Although at that time a ten-hour day had been secured in the middle

54

Atlantic states for children in several lines of work, the New Englanders still clung tenaciously to the more profitable system with the argument that "the morals of the operatives will necessarily suffer if longer absent from the wholesome discipline of factory life." Commenting upon this point of view, Mr. Adams asks, "Could Puritan hypocrisy go farther?"

However the authentic Puritan may have suffered from the loose attribution of varied qualities to his nature, the popular connotation of the term "puritan conscience," in both its brutal and its humorous aspects, remains clear enough in the minds of most Americans. Glenway Westcott's *The Grandmothers* describes a patriarchal character, a hypochondriac, who was constantly a prey to the vague promises of patent medicines. For a time a small closet downstairs was given over to his treasured remedies; later, as he added copiously to his store of pill bottles and assorted bottles, it was necessary to devote an entire room upstairs to his healing pellets and lotions. When these quarters were beginning to seem cramped and inadequate, the old man, to the relief of the family, fell into a deep cynicism on the subject of patent medicines. He then, according to Mr. Westcott, found relief only in Duffy's Malt Whiskey, which he took by the teaspoonful—he being a total abstainer!

This agreeably flexible attitude of mind I take as a perfect embodiment of the puritan conscience. It demands a moral justification of conduct, albeit the purity of the spirit may be established through devious and evasive lines of reasoning. The three hundred and seventy-three pages of text and the two hundred and twenty-three pages of notes by means of which Professor Kittredge's *Witchcraft in Old and New England* suffocates the suspicion that the American Puritan bears responsibility for the Salem massacres in 1692 may free the Puritan somewhat from the superstitious butchery associated with his name, but the far more subtle and more interesting imputation of popular usage still insists that "puritanical" connotes an inevitable demand for moral justification through a process of reasoning frequently specious.

From the European analogy of the last century we have the expression "Victorian conscience." Alfred Lord Tennyson may be accepted as the prime manifestation of this phenomenon. The damsel at her spinning wheel in the tower in Tennyson's "The Lady of Shalott" has vowed that she will cast no direct glance from her window, but apparently it is allowable for her to peer indirectly by means of the reflections in her mirror. Her sin, which brings sorrowful death, is committed only when she looks directly forth upon Lancelot; the mirror, representing an evasive path toward the same end, is then mystically shattered.

After much meditation, I think it fair to say that a

primary urge towards moral justification, in the absence of "outside critics," is not a marked feature of the southern conscience. Characteristically, the southerner acts intuitively. He not often deems a simple rationalization necessary before his head can rest easily upon the pillow; his moral rectitude normally requires no constant bolstering up through tedious vindication of his conduct and desires. He trusts native patterns. Nothing more clearly demonstrates how near the ante-bellum South came to formulating an integrated culture than the fact that to this day the individual ethics and morality of her descendants should be submerged in a larger and inclusive social consciousness. As respecting slavery, drinking whiskey, and a state of class inequality, the southerner—left to himself—felt no moral obloquy; these things were included in the social order, for which he had complete respect.

The southern conscience is unruffled by the act of lifting a glass with one hand and gesturing for prohibition with the other; the puritan conscience, however, would require a fragile explanation such as "What I am able to do with impunity would be injurious to weaker souls." As a matter of fact, the South believes in prohibition much less as a moral principle than as a political instrument. The spectacle of a dry South, along with other and similar anomalies, must be viewed in the light of catastrophic changes which have attended the inevitable adjustment of the old régime to a new order which is as yet inchoate and undetermined. Important among these changes is the present ascendancy of popular government.

When the Populist parties essayed a stand against the former powers in the South, moral principles offered a convenient vehicle for revolt. Somewhat the same state of affairs attended the English uprising led by Oliver Cromwell. The Populists were first identified with the Anti-Saloon League; later, with the revived Ku Klux Klan. The economic motivation present in the Grangers, Greenbackers, Free Silverites, Non-Partisan Leaguers, Farmer-Laborites, and Progressives of the Middle West was but vaguely apparent in the southern phase of the same general movement. Thus it is that what appears in the present-day South as moral or religious fanaticism— by which I mean to indicate zeal for prohibition and anti-Catholic bombast—is in reality political radicalism. It represents a misguided social revolution. The recent controversy in the Alabama legislature over near-beer statutes, which amused the nation, was fundamentally political, not moral or religious, in significance.

If the South had actually possessed even a mild form of religious fanaticism or a more decided moral consciousness, there would have been many more divisions of religious thought than a backward glance discloses in the region. When one has named the Episcopalians, the

Presbyterians, the Methodists, and the Baptists, he has encompassed the list of widely distributed and influential coteries. Profound delving into the conscience produces a separation into many cults. Unitarians, Christian Scientists, Quakers, Seventh Day Adventists, Lutherans, Mormons, Spiritualists, Congregationalists, and Catholics are few and far between in the South. In spite of its reputation for revivals and evangelism, the South has not yet toed the mark with a Billy Sunday, an Aimee McPherson, or a Wilbur Glenn Voliva, although it has given Sam Jones, Gypsy Smith, and Rattlesnake Teester to the world. Except for the misleading political manifestations which have been mentioned, serious and soul-stirring rivalry among the sects has never flourished in the South. Normally the various denominations are not violently competitive. Among the Baptists, for instance, there is the pleasant saying that anyone can be an Episcopalian, since the tenets of that church never interfere with one's religion.

At the same time, it is true that southern conduct with respect to ethics and religion has now and then chilled the marrow of some outside observers, who, if the truth be known, do not like southerners very well anyway. To such adverse critics, the southerner is generally content to state simply that outsiders do not understand him. Southern assurance is not always a pose; it often is a real quality, one tangible enough to cause a kind of frustrated

rage to burn in the hearts of those who have tried to pene-
trate the armor of a civilization which in its time has
come very close to being definitive.

2

A few years ago the world buzzed with indignation
over a certain abortive trial in Dayton, Tennessee, at
which Mr. Clarence Darrow and Mr. William Jennings
Bryan furnished a grotesque spectacle to an audience
which gasped and shuddered anew for many days as the
newspapers milled fresh evidence of religious bigotry
and abysmal ignorance in the Tennessee back country.
After the world had subsided somewhat from the shock
of appalling discovery, its agreeable smugness was punc-
tured a bit by an article appearing in *Harper's Magazine*
under the title, "Why Pick on Dayton?" The author
contended that the "monkey trial" might have taken
place in almost any other part of the United States as
well as at Dayton. He named the personalities of Mr.
Darrow and Mr. Bryan as the basis for dramatic conflict,
and held that the environment had been a nonessential
element in the performance. One might go further in
this direction with the assertion that a location in Kansas,
Ohio, or Indiana, where larger auditoriums and hotels
and better railroad connections would have been available, might have done even better by the venders of hamburger sandwiches. Nebraska, after all, has first claim

to Mr. Bryan. New York guardians of liberty might
have saved railroad fare and voluminous perspiration by
setting the measurably dubious scholarship of Mr. Darrow against the ardor of their own Dr. John Roach
Straton.

Mr. Darrow and Mr. Bryan, nevertheless, were contending over a law passed by the state of Tennessee; the
native population was spiritually involved on the side of
Mr. Bryan and was consequently a party to the argument. When the shrewd lawyers of the Chicago *Tribune*
chortled over Mr. Henry Ford's lack of elementary education—in that celebrated case which gave rise to Mr.
Ford's fretful declaration that "history is bunk"—no
derogation attached to the city of Detroit or to the state
of Michigan, even when court evidence sustained the
Tribune's forthright characterization of their god as an
"ignoramus." But the gimlet questions and ironic sneers
of the sallow Mr. Darrow were taken as indictments of
the state of Tennessee, and indeed of the entire South,
by most of those who sniffed at poor Mr. Bryan's un-
familiarity with Biblical text. Those who sensed that the
entire South was involved were correct in such an assumption; but they were wholly incorrect in their tacit
conclusion that the basis for conflict was a quarrel between science and religion isolated from broader con-
tiguous phenomena.

Here was no mortal combat in which soul and intellect

wrestled in bitter throes over a controversial theological dogma. Here was no racking debate such as those which stirred the mediaeval scholastics, or which furrowed the brow of Ralph Waldo Emerson or tortured the spirit of Jonathan Edwards. The Tennessee people were threatened by an alien force, which sought to destroy their self-determination. Led by certain of their own people, whom they trusted without argument, they had placed on their statute books, without great ado, a certain law which seemed to conserve the integrity of their customs, a law protecting the churches about which their social patterns, their essential culture, foregathered to an important extent. One may safely assume that their knowledge of theological dogma and of ecclesiastical systems was as loose and scattered as that of Mr. Bryan. Unfamiliar with the weapons of philosophical contention, and not particularly interested in the paraphernalia of abstract reasoning, they nevertheless clearly understood that foreign bodies of explosive power were being hurled into the midst of a social order which they enjoyed, cherished, and were determined to maintain.

Granting at once that their showing, through their champion, was inglorious on the strange plane where the fantasy was enacted, it remains obvious that their immediate victory was complete on the plane where their fundamental interests and concerns naturally rested. When in answer to Mr. Darrow's sneering thrusts Mr.

Bryan was content to repeat, "I believe it if it's in the
Bible," the native audience echoed assent, for to them
such a statement was equivalent to their real sentiment:
"We care little for the terms of your argument and less
for what your estimate of us may be. We should thank
you for non-interference; but if you insist upon argument, we are willing to return conventional answers to
everything you put forward, until you tire of the
monotony and go away."

If any lesson is to be learned from a retrospective glance
at the Dayton trial, if it can be regarded as more than
an isolated and spectacular performance, one observer
might point towards religious bigotry, ignorance, and
stubborn fundamentalism. Another analysis might disclose a people fighting for a whole civilization. If this
second conception suggests the manner in which the rôle
of religion is integrated with the larger cultural aspects
of present-day life in the South, then one may have cause
to suspect that religion in parts of the southern states has
been invalidated as a positive force tending to correct the
apparent social evils. Furthermore, there are some
grounds for thinking that the pulpit and the pew are
indeed so well integrated with the southern culture that
they have become, in too many instances, powerful factors in support of southern complacency and resistance
to social improvement, especially when foreign influences are concerned. Is it, after all, necessary for

science to be southern—for plans looking towards the improvement of society and the increase of human happiness to be southern—before they can be understood and accepted in the South?

3

In his stimulating essay entitled "Remarks on the Southern Religion," Allen Tate writes in a manner so casual that the reader is likely to overlook the depths of his implications. He advances the revealing observation that the southerner's religion is uncodified mainly because the southerner has been satisfied to rely upon what Thomas Jefferson conceived as a "sense of taste." Mr. Tate believes, if I interpret him correctly, that the South has lost an opportunity to embody its essential tradition in a systematized religion, and that, having done so, the present possibilities of consolidating a body of tradition are dependent upon the instrument of politics.

Agreeing with Mr. Tate that the South has never derived a positive and vigorous religious code suited to its peculiar characteristics, one may at the same time discern that several practices and points of view touching upon religion have been peculiar to this region. For instance, church-going has been much more a part of the purely social life in the South than in other areas of the United States. When Mr. Tate says that the "professional man of religion" these days in the South seems to "speak from

A courthouse evangelist. In spite of its reputation for revivals and evangelism, the South has not yet toed the mark with a Billy Sunday, an Aimee McPherson, or a Wilbur Glenn Voliva, although it has given Sam Jones, Gypsy Smith, and Rattlesnake Teester to the world.

A southern mansion now used as the library of Stillman Institute, a school for Negroes in Tuscaloosa, Alabama.

the tripod" less than he formerly did, I should not be sure that he is correct were it not for my confidence in him as a competent historian. Cases which have fallen under my observation lead me to believe that a fervor often to be identified with religious emotionalism is frequently to be remarked in the politics, business enterprises, and communal promotions of the present-day South. When Mr. Tate, speaking of the authoritative position formerly held by the southern minister in his relationships with the layman who inclined towards philosophy, says that "we have none of that respect now," I am privately of the opinion that he could not display his slate throughout the South without numerous awkward misgivings.

Rivaled in his position as undisputed center of the social structure, the southern minister has often strengthened his authority by cultivating secular relationships in order to meet the new economics on neutral ground. The slipper of the Anglican divine moves in earnest grace across the ballroom floor at country clubs, and the heavier foot of the Calvinist regularly marks the turf on many a putting green. Any slackening of the churchward procession in recent years has been compensated by a concourse of ministers around the festive noontide board of Kiwanis. Mohammed has gone to the mountain.

If the South has been indisposed towards systematizing its conscience in the form of an indigenous religious creed, its use of the church has been stamped with an emphasis upon broadly social values rather than upon an intellectualization of morals. The predominantly rural character of the South has greatly influenced such a tendency. Religion and secular life have exerted reciprocal influences because the church usually has been the place for social gatherings. Even at barbecues, political rallies, and county fairs the people are likely to wear their Sunday clothes, and there is often a certain grave suggestion of church manners and inflections at such gatherings.

In the rural districts and small communities of the South the church has been the center of most socialized forms of artistic experience. It is there that the people have heard nearly all the music which has entered their lives. From the juvenile tunes attending the dropping of pennies in the cradle-roll class to the solemn dirges accompanying the fall of fresh earth on the grave, church songs are the ones which they have whistled or hummed at work or play; and pianos in their homes have seldom vibrated to the measures of any music except that of the hymnal. What the introduction of popular dance songs and musical comedy hits by the radio will bring about cannot be predicted with certainty, but I suspect that it will tend to show that the former selection of church music was dictated by a limit in choice as much as by devout preference. A similar question now hangs between church attendance and movie patronage. Whatever of oratory, stagecraft, inspiration, literature, emotional experience, and exaltation one enjoyed in the rural South twenty years ago was likely to be centered in a large measure in the church. Comparatively well educated, mysterious, and remote, the minister was impressive as being the only man in the community who regularly spoke in public, read books, and performed in a setting conducive to drama and imaginative pleasure.

While secret lodges gave men some touches of mysticism, symbolism, and ritual, the church was the only place where all might gather for the exercise of those functions which in urban communities are interspersed among libraries, concert halls, theaters, lecture halls, colleges, and art galleries. If artistic life was largely involved with the church, moral and philosophical considerations were even more so. The tenet that all good citizens must be churchgoers was hardly assailable, for nonattendance labelled one as antisocial, unmoral, unimaginative, inartistic, or dull. If in the South a few strictly urban communities have made their appearance within recent years, most of the inhabitants of them still carry the imprints of previous experience sufficiently to create a strong feeling that the church is the most tangible embodiment of idealism, aspiration, consolation, and morality. I have noted that the speeches of Rotarians, professors, and politicians in the South are rarely so secular as not to adumbrate the tone and gesture of ministerial utterance.

4

When that wave of religious fervor known as the
Great Awakening swept the United States during the
second quarter of the eighteenth century, the South was
involved less than were other regions, although George
Whitefield labored for a while in the south Atlantic states.
Perhaps this was not so much because of the lack of religious feeling in the South as because of the fact that the
form and structure of a unified society had already been
determined in this section. The southern conscience had
previously been absorbed into an inclusive entity; consequently it was less subject to influence as an isolated
aspect of regional consciousness. The thunderous echoes
of Jonathan Edwards, John Wesley, and George Whitefield were mostly felt in the New England and middle Atlantic states. When the righteous Edwards was playing
a dismal Emily Post to moral conduct, the South was
more intent upon raising the price of cotton. Respecting
the morality of taking food, Edwards wrote as follows
in his diary on the Saturday night of February 15, 1724:
"I find that when eating, I cannot be convinced in the
time of it, that if I should eat more, I should exceed the
bounds of strict temperance, though I have had the experience of two years of the like; and yet, as soon as I
have done, in three minutes I am convinced of it. But
yet, when I eat again, and remember it, still, while eating, I am fully convinced that I have not eaten what

is but for nature, nor can I be convinced that my appetite and feeling is as it was before. It seems to me that I shall be somewhat faint if I leave off then; but when I have finished, I am convinced again, and so it is from time to time." Without offense to the good Edwards, a southerner might wonder whether personal morality and temperance might not exist without such agony of conscience and prose style. Confronted by the same momentous question while eating dinner, perhaps the southerner, even in 1724, had contrived to express the point succinctly and with less pious fustian, giving rise to a regional proverb: "Always leave the table feeling that you could eat another biscuit."

It is by no means my contention that the South has lacked an awareness of God, or that southern people have failed to worship Him in a spirit of sincerity and humility. And it would be a serious mistake for one to infer that the South has not been uplifted and exhorted to apply Christianity to its problems by many courageous and inspiring ministers of the gospel. Yet, the noble examples set by these consecrated and intelligent preachers are not always sufficient to overweigh the lassitude with which so many of the members of their congregations, as well as so many of their colleagues, are inclined to look upon social evils that need correction. Six years ago a well-educated, attractive, and earnest young Episcopal minister—himself a Virginian—came from Boston to take a

parish in a college town of the deep South. He had as-
siduously schooled himself to meet a rising tide of religious skepticism. His problem, however, was at the same
time both alleviated and magnified when he found, upon
arrival, that the tide had not risen. Such experiences as
this must prove discouraging to the very type of religious
leader who could, with adequate support, give vitality to
the doctrines of Jesus at this time in the South.

Edmund Wilson, writing a few years ago in *The New
Republic*, declared that the early slave master accepted
without evasion the moral implications of his acts; that,
as a consequence, the southerner today has a right to be
suspicious of "the northerner's principles and preten-
sions—smelling hypocrisy in his human anxieties, mania
in his moral idealism, and in his eternal insistence upon
'service' a compensation for the savageries of a society
predatory and egoistic in the extreme." While not convinced that Mr. Wilson has photographed the plight of
southern charity with absolute exactitude, one must
thank him for a left-handed compliment. But has Mr.
Wilson not had the benefit of reading some of the documents drawn up by the southern slave masters when they
were protecting themselves against the activities of the
Abolitionists? Then there is a list of similar documents
drawn up during the later period of "white control" and
"white supremacy." Charles S. Johnson's *The Negro in
American Civilization* cites one of these from the pen of

Judge Benjamin Tillman, of Quitman, Georgia. It follows: "The Negro bears about him a birthright of inferiority that is as unalterable as eternity. He who, in the morning of Creation, set the shifting sands as a barrier to the mad waves of the mighty deep and said thus far, has also set his seal upon the Negro forever in his black skin, kinky hair, thick lips, flat nose, double layer of skull, different anatomy, as well as analogy, from white men. His stupid intellect is fulfilled in prophecy, uttered thousands of years ago, but no less true today, 'A servant of servants shalt thou be'." When all is said and done, after considering both rhetoric and substance, could one reasonably expect more of the puritan conscience than that?

Chapter V
Politics as a Major Sport

I

FOR some years I have been harboring the ridiculous notion that articles on election campaigns in the South, as well as all partisan editorials on the subject, should be printed on the sports pages of the newspapers. To the full enjoyment of politics as a major sport, at any rate, the southern conscience offers no impediment. In truth, I find myself corroborated in this philistine attitude by no less an authority than the leading newspaper published at the first capital of the Confederacy. Even in the midst of a furious state campaign in 1934, the Montgomery *Advertiser* found itself able to preserve perspective in the following manner: "The boys are getting hot under the collar, which means, in all probability, a heavy vote on June 12. But let them keep their shirts on. . . . The destiny of the human race has never yet been determined by the outcome of a popular political campaign. . . . Enjoy the campaign, but take it easy, is the advice of a newspaper which has seen candidates come and go since a fair day in the springtime of 1828." A perfect example of a man who for a score of years ministered to the southerner's delight in the sport of politics may be descried in the career of J. Thomas Heflin.

Forty-one years ago a bumptious young rustic was appointed to a small clerkship at the courthouse of Chambers County in the stumpy hills and sun-baked red valleys of East Alabama. He was James Thomas Heflin at the age of twenty-four. Having already overwhelmed the rural environs of his boyhood, he had sought a new afflatus in the county-seat town of Lafayette, and, expanding there his talents as a show-off, he soon emerged as Sir Oracle again. His world was not the moth-eaten record books and the high stool that cramped his active body. He preferred to loiter in the dim and acrid corridors, roaring crafty badinage and slapping the backs of the country people who sat propped for hours on their haunches, lolling their quids of tobacco from tongue to cheek and talking about cotton and the coming election.

Passing through the hallways month after month and seeing the knots of people always gathered about this guffawing young clerk, Probate Judge Driver, a whip-horse of the Democratic party, one day ushered Heflin into private consultation. That was in 1895. The "rise of the people" had reached Alabama; there was loud clamor for a division of the Democratic party. Calling themselves Jeffersonians, while their enemies termed them Populists (or, more commonly, *Populites*), the small farmers and under-privileged classes were banding together to push their own candidates into office. There was a pressing need for leaders whose characteristics would appeal to the revolutionists and steer them back into the fold. Young Heflin seemed perfectly adapted for such a post.

The next year the regular Democrats backed him for the state legislature. Stumping his district, he thus referred to his opponent, an insurgent candidate: "He's no bigger than a bump on a pine log. If he gets down there to Montgomery, he'll buy a bag of peanuts and put one of them on his desk so the speaker of the house won't be able to see him." The indignant rejoinder was: "If you stick a pitchfork in Tom Heflin and let the wind blow out, a pair of my breeches would swallow him." Heflin won the race without any difficulty whatever. Subsequently he remained in public office continuously for thirty-five years.

In 1930 the enlightened elements of the Democratic party in Alabama—consisting partially of a liberal-minded and progressive group of the new generation— determined to end Old Tom's political career. His mad rush upon Al Smith in 1928 had piled up 120,000 Alabama votes for Herbert Hoover, while the regular Democrats had strained their last ounce of energy in retaining 127,000 votes for the party nominees. As a consequence, the state Democratic executive committee banned Heflin from entering the party primaries in August of 1930. This action was bitterly contested, and the opponents of Heflin won by a majority of only six ballots in a vote of forty-eight members.

Cotton Tom accepted the challenge. First he called upon the committee to rescind their action. "We have fallen upon strange times," he bellowed. "The story is going around that money was used in that committee. When money from the Roman Pope and Tammany Hall can corrupt the sovereign state of Alabama, it is time for decent men to take a hand. The story is told that the liquor jug was flowing freely down there at Montgomery. The aged father of one of the members told me the boys never would have slaughtered me without a trial if they hadn't been drunk. They desecrated the Sabbath as well, while they were holding that week-end orgy." Realizing that they had played somewhat into the hands of Heflin by furnishing him with a powerful persecution motif, the committee for a time wavered. In the end, however, the majority held firm.

2

Campaigning in this crisis, Heflin relied upon his unvarying formula with the Alabama voter: the raucous tale, with mimicry of Negro or rural characters, followed by an irrelevant interpretation in terms of whatever issues might be pressing at the moment. The convulsed assemblage was never a stickler for precise logical progression.

One time, roared Heflin, lifting his fat chin to the side and twinkling his rather glassy eyes, a party was fishing and hunting in the swamps of Louisiana. "Down there they call swamps bye-yous," he explained. "While paddling around in a boat, they came opposite a clearing where somebody lived, and they stopped awhile to watch a flock of fifteen or twenty little niggers playing around on the bank. Suddenly they saw one of those big slimy crocodiles glide in there, catch up one of the little niggers, and swallow him down. Dashing to the edge of the clearing, the fishermen came upon an old Negro mammy, who was busily washing clothes in a boiler and hanging them out to dry. Hearing of the tragic occurrence, she began to count the numerous brood now scurrying about her skirts. 'Lawdy, Lawdy,' she moaned. 'Ain't I done been tellin' Andy dat somebody's been a-stealin' dem chillun!' " Amid the resultant avalanche of laughter, Heflin pounded the rostrum and shook his great red fist in the air. "What I mean to tell you is that something's been a-stealin' the chillun of Democracy. Maybe you don't know what that something is. I'm here to tell you it's the tainted dollars of the Roman Pope."

On July 4 Heflin announced the resurrection of the Jeffersonians to fight the regular Democratic candidates in the general election scheduled for November. The Jeffersonians planned to hold their own primaries in every county on August 12, the same day as the regular primaries, and they announced a general convention of their forces to be held in Montgomery in September, in

anticipation of the general election in November. In addition to the Jeffersonians, there was a Heflin legion; the
legionnaires bought memberships at $2.00 each, and pre-
sumably swore eternal allegiance to Old Tom. With
characteristic evasion, Heflin declaimed, "We have no
third party. The party of Thomas Jefferson has fallen
into strange hands. We are going to give it back to the
rank and file of the Democratic people, where it belongs."

John H. Bankhead, the son of the first Senator John H.
Bankhead, to whose unexpired term Heflin succeeded
when he was first elected to the Senate in 1920, was
Heflin's opponent in November. Thus Cotton Tom, late
in his career of many contradictions, at last led the forces
of insurrection, against which he was pitted when saga-
cious party members in 1895 snatched him from his clerkship in the Chambers County courthouse and sent him
to the state legislature.

In the speaking campaign, Heflin laid violent stress
upon the issues of 1928, for he wished to capture the
120,000 anti-Smith votes in Alabama. Towards this end
he interpreted the favorite old story of the early days of
the telephone. "When these telephone people were first
trying to buy up tracts of land so they could set up their
rural lines, they couldn't persuade Uncle Johnny to listen
to reason," Heflin began. "All Uncle Johnny would say
was, 'I'm agin 'em.' They tried to explain just how the

contraption worked. 'Do you mean to tell me yer words goes along of them thar little wires?' Uncle Johnny asked. 'Is them wires hollow? If they ain't hollow, why don't them words fall offen the wires? An' why don't the rain wash 'em off?'

"Finally they got the old man in town one day and made a connection with his wife in a little place about ten miles away. 'Come on now, Uncle Johnny,' they said, 'an' talk to yer old woman.' 'Is she in that 'ere little box?' Uncle Johnny wanted to know. They pushed him up to the telephone, in spite of his protests, and put the receiver to his ear. Just then there came a streak of lightning and a big thunder clap. Uncle Johnny was struck. As he fell back five feet and began to crawl under a table, he yelled out, 'That's her all right—that shore is my old woman!'"

As soon as his voice could be heard above the uproar, Heflin continued, "Now you can't blame old Uncle Johnny for being a little skeptical when he first heard about that mysterious telephone, and I can't blame you for wanting proof about some of the things I'm telling you. It takes a stroke of lightning to wake up some people. Well, back of the strange doings of Al Smith and his friend Raskob is their master's voice in the Vatican at Rome. They are getting ready for another attempt in 1932."

3

The profound significance of the expression "I'm agin it" in southern folk psychology is worth a passing note. The words indicate a defense mechanism against any condition which the people feel to be mysterious, suspicious, and consequently menacing to them. The attitude is widely characteristic. It serves to explain in part the dread of the Catholic church. There are no Catholics whatever in many southern towns; many of the country people have never seen a priest or a nun. Yet, when they are told of the rituals and symbolisms of the Catholics, they feel that there is something devilish, witch-like, and ominous about it all. "What's them critters garbed up like that fer?—What's they a-hatchin' up in thar?" The Catholic procedure is utterly bewildering and terrorizing. To a limited degree the attitude is directed against Episcopalians. With the recent slight ingressions of competitive labor in the form of Italian, Irish, and Mexican Catholics, the agitation against the religion of the foreigner has assumed a new economic basis.

Heflin had at least one other major grievance against the regular Democrats. They stole his thunder relative to "white supremacy" and the glory of the "white man's party." Indeed, it was only through appeal to the mythical dread of the Emperor Jones that the Democrats were able to offset the temporary menace of Romanism in

1928. Nevertheless, in 1930 Heflin continued to make capital of the helpless white man's fear and jealousy of Negro competition.

His deliberate flatteries of the poor white man's somewhat doubtful sense of superiority over the Negro were both cunning and devious. At the beginning of one of his addresses in a crowded auditorium, the master of ceremonies, presumably at Heflin's direction, rose with a troubled countenance. "I understand," he said, "that there are a lot of Negro men occupying good seats in the back of this hall. There are some white southern ladies down here who are being compelled to stand up. Black people, get up and give these white ladies your seats." (Heflin, incidentally, gave no prominence to the recorded fact that he voted against the woman suffrage amendment in the United States House of Representatives in 1919.) Careful scrutiny of the auditorium disclosed only one Negro in the entire assembly; he was standing, embarrassed and out of place, near the main doorway. The effect, nevertheless, was unhampered. On a previous occasion in Washington Heflin had cried, "If that Negro, DePriest, comes in the barber shop while I'm there, I'll punch him in the jaw"; in Birmingham, shortly thereafter, a thousand men dressed in Ku Klux Klan regalia burned DePriest in effigy.

All the characters and episodes of Mr. Heflin's tales were close to the life experiences of his followers. A

A hill-country chair-maker splitting logs with a mallet and a wedge.

Making chair rockers. In the hilly sections of Georgia, Alabama, Tennessee, and the Carolinas, the number of handicraft products for sale in small communities and along the highways has visibly increased during the past two years.

much-repeated story dealt with a backwoodsman's first contact with a mirror. The itinerant salesman was able to overcome the mountaineer's superstitious dread only by telling him that the image in the glass was a picture of his grandfather. "I'm agin it," the mountaineer averred. At last, however, he purchased the mysterious object and carried it home. Not daring to show it to his wife, he hid the magic frame under a pile of hay in the barn loft. Regularly he would trail from the house and gaze for long periods into its depths.

His wife, becoming suspicious, followed him to the barn one day. Slipping up behind him, she seized the mirror and held it close to her face. "So this," she cried in a great rage, "is the old hussy you been a-sneakin' off out here to see every day." Heflin's interpretation was that the "old hussy" back of the political situation in Alabama was Tammany Hall.

Old Tom related that a stranger in a certain rural district was visiting an old man who lived by himself. Noticing a series of ten or twelve holes bored through the wall near the floor, the stranger inquired what they were. "Them's cat holes," the old man said. "Cat holes?" the stranger answered in surprise. "Why do you need ten or twelve of them? Ain't one hole enough? Don't all them make hit powerful drafty in here?" "Mebbe you don't understand, stranger," the old man explained, "but them cats do. They knows that when I says 'Scat!' I means

scat!" Drawing himself up proudly and waving his arms
belligerently in a sweeping gesture, Heflin declaimed,
"And these Raskobites and traitorous hirelings know that
when I say 'Scat!' I mean *scat!*"

4

As a youthful legislator, first in the Alabama Assembly
and then in the state Senate, Heflin had already begun
to affect eccentricities in speech and appearance. He was
to be marked by his sombrero hat, his high standing collar, the fantastic sash of a bow tie around his neck, and
his booming voice. To his friends he said a public man
ought to dress so the people would know him.

The son of a country physician struggling through the
lean days of the Civil War, Tom Heflin was born at the
crossroads settlement of Louina, near the village of Lafayette, in 1869. The old family home is still to be seen,
rambling and time-worn, and the countryside is invited
there annually to attend the reunion of the Heflin family.
In this family, besides Cotton Tom, there are a circuit
judge, a city physician, two Methodist preachers, and a
sister.

The Heflin brothers in a body attended country school
at Milltown, where, as a schoolmate testifies, they were
known far and wide as "those mean Heflin boys." Later
Tom attended Southern University, a kind of semi-
religious institution then conducted at Greensboro by a

state branch of the Methodist church. His formal school-
ing was concluded by a period at a polytechnic institute
located at Auburn, about twenty miles from Lafayette.
Not being inclined, however, to the pursuit of scholarship, Tom returned to his home. In a haphazard manner
he obtained a smattering of law, and was admitted to the
bar in 1893. Though his purely political career was begun
the very next year, Heflin likes to speak of himself as a
"professional" man.

During his four years at the capitol in Montgomery,
there were few warehouses available for the cotton
brought into town by the farmers. The bales were temporarily piled in long rows up and down the center of
Dexter Avenue. As Heflin walked daily from his hotel
to the capitol, he would hear the cotton buyers making
their bids to the farmers, and at night he would hear the
Negroes laughing and telling stories to each other as they
stood guard over the cotton bales throughout the warm
autumn nights. At this period Heflin began to think of
his political appeal in terms of cotton prices, and from
that time until 1924 he—bearing the name of Cotton
Tom—based all his speeches upon promises to obtain
higher prices for the main crop of the state.

Just how he was to influence this complicated economic process he never felt called upon to elucidate. If
he ever did anything whatever toward such an end, the
record has failed to bear witness. On occasions, however,

when the quotations happened to be on the rise, he found it easy to convince his untutored audiences that he alone was their benefactor. Contrary conditions he met by blaming the farmers for not holding their cotton for a favorable market, as he had repeatedly advised them to do. That a tenant farmer, with an average cash income of $10 a month, cannot well hold his cotton, when the crop is heavily mortgaged before being planted, is a consideration for which Heflin assumed no logical responsibility.

Precisely when Senator Heflin ceased to be exclusively "Cotton Tom" and became mainly a crusader against the Pope cannot be determined with certainty. His split with the party came in 1924. When it appeared that his old friend, ex-Governor W. W. Brandon, might oppose him for the Senate, he exclaimed, "You kind of expect a fice dog to follow around after a big Newfoundland." His particular antipathy and jealousy, however, were directed against his senior colleague, Senator Oscar W. Underwood. When Underwood announced against the Ku Klux Klan in preparation for the national Democratic convention in New York, Heflin is supposed to have determined deliberately that he would cast his lot with that organization.

In Alabama it is often said that Heflin sometimes received surprisingly large fees for his addresses to the Klansmen. On the days when he made public addresses,

the newspapers often carried large notices of Klan gatherings to hear a "distinguished visiting member." Conjecture was that the notable thus thinly veiled was obviously
Heflin. At any rate, he was never heard to speak pub-
licly against the Catholics in Alabama before 1924, one
of the years in which the Klan was particularly active.
His closest friends uniformly attest his lack of originality.
It seems, therefore, quite plausible that, finding himself
adrift from the party and without the counsels of his
former advisers, he took over bodily the general platform
of the Ku Klux Klan and steered his course accordingly.
At this time he viciously attacked the wet stand of Senator Underwood, regardless of the record that he himself
voted against the national prohibition amendment in the
United States House of Representatives in 1917. When
President Coolidge rebuked him for introducing religious controversy into the Senate, and when Senator Joe
Robinson of Arkansas bitterly assailed him for the same
affront, the undirected emotionalism of Heflin appears
to have been fanned into a venomous and consuming fury.

5

Without achieving a reputation for industry as a states-
man, and indeed without particular concern for details
of public affairs except as they touched his personal
career, young Heflin loafed through his two terms in the
state legislature. Often until the small hours of the morn-

ing he would sit with several cronies in a room at the Exchange Hotel or Joseph's Restaurant. Upon the table, covered with a faded piece of drapery, they would place bills scheduled for debate in the legislature. One of the company would take a gavel and act as presiding officer. "I recognize the gentleman from Chambers," he would say. Then Heflin would rise and deliver the speech which he had prepared. The others would offer criticisms and suggestions, and later they would present their own addresses, under the flickering gas lights. Heflin was said to lack an ability for original thought; yet he could repeat without a blunder long passages which he had read and others which his friends had composed for him. Mainly distinguished as a mimic, he could bark like a dog, crow like a rooster, and croon like a violin.

His model in those days was the grotesque Bob Taylor, governor of Tennessee. With his photographic memory, Heflin was able to reproduce whole speeches of Taylor's, and he delighted to imitate that odd character's mannerisms through long stanzas of "The Fiddle and the Bow." Another model for the group was the flamboyant orator, Samuel D. Prentice, of Mississippi. Heflin would memorize the meaningless rhetoric of Prentice and run whole passages into his own speeches, with complete irrelevance. One such passage dealt with "tearing the stars from the flag of Mississippi and leaving the stripes as a token of her shame." This figure Heflin transferred to

Alabama and used it in supporting or opposing bills on the floor, to the stupefied admiration of his colleagues.

To each other the members of the little group confided their ambitions and pledged mutual support. Heflin and one of his confidants were to go to Washington as representatives, and another was to be governor of Alabama. They planned astute tricks to help each other. If constituents of one of the group came to Montgomery on business, the visitors would be carefully installed in a room next to the one where the cronies were to meet. At night three of the legislators would carefully declaim speeches laudatory of the other member, whose constituents could hear every word through the thin partition walls of the hotel. The effect was electric.

"For God's sake, let me in there with old John," bellowed Tom-Tom Heflin in his campaign against Mr. Bankhead in 1930. "Why, John hasn't got any more chance to go to the United States Senate than a mouse-colored mule has to operate an airplane!" But John H. Bankhead did go to the United States Senate, although he could not take his seat until an official investigation of the election returns, carried through upon Heflin's demand, had cost the government many thousands of dollars. As for Heflin, he retired to Lafayette, where he met his sympathetic friends daily at Collins' Drug Store. In 1934 he ran for a seat in Congress, and was defeated. Before doing so, however, he had offered his talents in

the prosecution of several Negroes supposedly intoxi-
cated with Red propaganda and had suggested that James
E. Horton, the liberal judge, be removed from jurisdiction in the Scottsboro case. Upon the announcement of
the election returns in 1934, poor Mr. Heflin issued the
following statement: "My friends wanted to contest the
primary election in the sixteen precincts in question in
DeKalb County. I have informed them that . . . I would
endure the wrong done me and accept the results of the
official count." Possibly the defeat of Heflin may indicate
the appearance of a more serious attitude towards government in the South. But such an interpretation would be
hazardous in view of the present ascendancy of Huey P.
Long and Theodore G. Bilbo.

Already the South has suffered enough from that irresponsibility which allows southern voters to treat politics
as a major sport. It was worth traveling a hundred miles
over bad roads to hear Tom Heflin speak. At the height
of his career he was able to draw huge audiences in
almost any part of the United States. Once in Chicago a
tremendous crowd presented him with a handsome diamond ornament in appreciation of his oratorical efforts.
But first-rate ability as a popular entertainer should not
be considered a prime qualification for high public office. People worthy of discharging the duties of citizenship cannot elect a man to the Senate simply because he
amuses them. Possibly the followers of such men as Hef-

lin, Long, and Bilbo have remained under the delusion that their champions are fighting the battles of the common people. But the tragedy implicit in this false confidence is that a demagogue has a way of promising the people everything and of getting them nothing. Glancing down the course of southern history, which leads through the careers of Jeff Davis of Arkansas (not the president of the Confederacy), the Taylors of Tennessee, Cole Blease of South Carolina, the Fergusons of Texas, "Alfalfa Bill" Murray of Oklahoma, and the three notables whom I have mentioned, one is almost forced to believe that a peculiar type of Fascism has been at work below the Potomac, although the southern states have not yet produced a Mussolini or a Hitler.

Chapter VI

Fascism: Southern Style

I

WHAT success the Americans will have in forcing their unripe standards upon the reluctant state of Mississippi, how long the battle will last, and what its consequences may reveal are subjects for exciting conjecture. For the state of Mississippi is a bulwark of passive resistance. It is a prey to internal desuetude; its power of expression, as it were, is held in abeyance between antiquity on the one hand and immaturity on the other. Most remote of the southern states from the present centers of kinetic radiation, it remains a neglected outpost of the quiet splendors of the old régime, while its comparative lack of industrial materials has presented no land of promise for the new.

Although many Americans in the midst of plenty are pursued by a paradoxical fear that they will be unable to make a livelihood from one day to the next, the Mississippians are singularly free from any such consuming dread. They are infidels in the fold of good business; they cling to an agnostic faith in a sort of irresponsibility which limits community endeavors. Everlasting familiarity with debt has bred in them a contempt for its power. Through years of direful conflict with mortgages, diminishing collateral, and foreclosures, the planters of the Mississippi delta have emerged at least moral victors. Even though the total value of agricultural products in the state sank to $134,460,000 in 1930, which was only 51 per cent of the corresponding figure ($262,469,000) for 1929—and while banks were closing their doors in disconcerting numbers—planters and tenants alike pursued the even tenor of their ways with remarkable equanimity. Nor did they in 1930 match the nation's somewhat intrusive concern with their own trepidations about educational conditions in Mississippi. Are there not some free spirits in America who, momentarily dropping their masks of conformity, are able to descry a quality of hardihood in these people; a sinewy stiffness of character which, if quixotic in a measure, is still not without a kind of stark and lonely grandeur in this docile world?

From the northwestern corner of Mississippi an elevated range extends directly southward through about two-thirds of the state; and at nearly the same point the great river, on its way from Memphis to New Orleans, bends slightly westward. The river and the mountainous range come together again near Vicksburg. Parts of about twelve western counties have been included in the region which they have enclosed, and this area is known as the delta. It has always been the dwelling place of "the quality." The land itself is of that rich loamy texture usually associated with delta areas; this results from the fact that

the immediate basin, or valley, of the river is extended
beyond its average width because the restraining mountains are here farther removed from the water. As well
as from the nature of the land, the region derives its name
also from the fact that the Yazoo River, which flows
along the western edge of the mountain range, empties
into the Mississippi River through a series of deltas just
above Vicksburg. Clarksdale, Greenville, Greenwood,
Hazelhurst, and Natchez are among the towns in the
favored area, while Jackson, which lies but the width of
two counties east of Vicksburg, marks the termination
of any feeling of kinship which the delta people cherish
for the remaining population of the state.

Of the seventy other counties in the state, about ten
are included in the prairie region. This area, which is
made up of softly rolling hills and rather grassy surfaces,
extends along the extreme eastern boundary. Aberdeen,
Columbus, and Meridian are towns in the prairie section,
while Laurel and Hattiesburg lie along the southwestern
edge of it. The inhabitants of this area lean somewhat in
sympathy towards the delta, but their basic interests and
pursuits are so different as to exclude any strong tie between the eastern and western extremities of the state.

In the southernmost counties, where Mississippi verges
into Louisiana on the southwest and protrudes a shelf into
the Gulf of Mexico on the southeast, the general tone of
life is colored by a mixture of influences, which lie rather

apart from the rest of the state. From Laurel and Hattiesburg down to the gulf coast there has been considerable
development of the long-leaf pine industries; aside from
the cutting of lumber, the manufacture of synthetic
wood and naval stores has been partly substituted for
single-minded dependence upon cotton. Pecans and vegetables for distant markets are also widely cultivated. The
beauty of the gulf coast itself and the suitability of the
waters of Mississippi Sound for swimming and fishing
have transformed a seventy-five-mile strip into a playground.

At Pass Christian, Gulfport, and Biloxi the shore is
lined with sumptuous vacation residences, which stand
far back from the beach in clusters of luxuriant trees hung
with festoons of Spanish moss. These places were originally the almost exclusive property of the delta folk; but
promotion campaigns in recent years have brought to
portions of Bay St. Louis and Biloxi suggestions of the
type of exploitation usually associated with Atlantic City.
Even so, this coast region has no special connection with
the rest of Mississippi. Most of its railroads lead to Mobile
and New Orleans, and travelers on that marvelous
thoroughfare, the Old Spanish Trail, seldom turn inland
at any of the Mississippi towns.

Between the delta and the prairie, and including all the
state north of the coastal plain, is that major portion of
Mississippi known as the hill country. The hills are not

marked geographical formations; but the slightly irregular contour of the land is exaggerated by comparison with the flatness of the delta, prairie, and coast. In the hill country live the great masses of the under-privileged people of the state. Their domain stretches over nearly three-fourths of the total area of Mississippi, and they compose an undisputed majority of the electorate. While farms of several thousand acres are the rule in the delta, the average size of farms in Mississippi as a whole in 1928 was 66.9 acres; and 66 per cent of all the farms in the state were operated by tenants. The small farms are generally in the hill country. Along with their struggles against the unfertile and eroding soil, the white men of the hill country have retained their old enmity against the Negro race, which composes more than one-half the population of the state in general and about four-fifths of the population of the delta.

To the hill folk the main trouble with education in Mississippi is that one is compelled by law to purchase textbooks for school children. Apparently oblivious to the statistics of the evangels of public education, representatives of these people gather at Jackson to hear with avidity the age-old complaints expressed by members of the Calvinistic clergy: "Millions of pagans are coming up in our public schools. . . . America is on its way to heathenism unless means can be provided to reach public school children with the Bible." Between hill and delta there have been natural differences which have seemed insurmountable. Much of the recent political, educational, and economic history of the state may be explained on grounds of these inevitable conflicts.

2

That movement in American history usually designated as "the rise of the common man" did not reach Mississippi until about 1890. Previous to that time the barons of the delta had ruled the state with unchallenged sovereignty. It was not that they craved political power. They were content with life within their own pleasant domain. With Memphis and New Orleans as their social and economic capitals, and in the security of their own principalities, they were far more interested in maintaining exclusiveness within their own borders than in extending their reach into the outside world. People of wide (but not scholarly) education, with taste, travel, and comparative wealth, they desired stability rather than change.

But unfortunately their economic system was too shallow to stand the test of time. Long ago their borrowings exhausted the resources of the state banks, and foreign capital was brought in. Money-lenders of obvious types amassed fortunes at the hands of the unwary planters. Today an English syndicate owns and operates a delta tract of eight thousand acres with the aim of making each acre yield a bale of that long-fiber cotton which brought a dollar a pound during the World War. To the native planters only the status of renter involved disgrace; the accumulation of debts, even to the point of final capitulation, could be borne with honor. And even at the moment when the prestige of the planters was tottering, there came to Mississippi the swelling shouts and challenging cries of the democratic rebellion.

The phase of resentment and revenge that identifies the present political period in Mississippi had its incipiency in the constitutional convention of 1890. At that time the masses of the people from the red-clay hill country first began to express their revolt against the English system of rule by the landowning classes. The governor's term was fixed at four years, and his reëlection for another consecutive term was made illegal. Provisions were made for a board of trustees, consisting of seven men appointed by the governor, to have absolute control of all matters pertaining to the three principal state educational institutions. Since, as a general rule, the tenure of one of the trustees expires each year, it has usually been possible for subsequent governors to obtain control of the board, through filling vacancies with their own appointees, during the last year of the gubernatorial term if not before.

Since the state colleges offer one of the most fruitful fields for patronage, it is only natural that recent governors should have taken advantage of their opportunities.

The country store, where politics is a major sport.

A load of fat pine kindling wood, "light'ood," on its way to market.

One must understand, of course, that scholarship and higher education as such have not built up in Mississippi any prestige which could make them sacrosanct against political pillage. School people in the state are always much concerned over their friends' losses of positions in the various colleges; but the implied assault upon the integrity of education and learning in the abstract is usually a bit beyond the field of their imagination.

3

The present political régime in Mississippi is generally thought of within the state as having been instituted by that amazing figure, James Kimble Vardaman. Mr. Vardaman was born in Texas in 1861; moving to Mississippi at an early age, he read law and was admitted to the Mississippi bar in 1882. He was without formal education and perhaps lacking in other special qualifications for social acceptance in the delta region where he settled. Into his columns of the *Enterprise*, which he edited at Greenwood, there began to creep suggestions of the social resentment and the iconoclastic method that were to come into full flower in his later career.

After establishing the *Commonwealth* at Greenwood, he two years later became editor of the *Issue*, a political organ published at Jackson. Already he had begun to hold a series of political posts in the state, having come into his first office in 1890, the year of the constitutional con-

vention which marked the rise of the hill people. Mr.
Vardaman was governor from 1904 to 1908 and United
States senator from 1913 to 1919. At Washington he was
distinguished in the public mind, first, because of his long
flowing hair (which he is said to have worn to conceal
a wen on the back of his neck), and, secondly, because of
his bitter stand with Senators Reed and La Follette against
the war policies of President Woodrow Wilson.

In Mississippi a frequent interpretation is that Mr.
Vardaman, while governor, formed a tacit alliance with
two younger men—Lee Maurice Russell and Theodore
Gilmore Bilbo. These were to constitute a triumvirate in
the new democracy of the state. A graduate of the University of Nashville, Mr. Bilbo studied law at Vanderbilt and Michigan. His lasting interest in the school system of Mississippi was possibly initiated during the years
immediately after his graduation, when he was a teacher
in the rural district schools. He has also served as a
preacher of an evangelical faith and as the editor of the
Mississippi Free Lance, a weekly political newspaper. As
a member of the law firm of Bilbo and Shipman, he established his permanent home in Poplarville, a village in the
lower hill country on one of the main railroads and highways to New Orleans. Entering public service in 1908,
he held state offices continuously for twelve years, including his first term as governor from 1916 to 1920.

Born at Oxford, the seat of the University of Mississippi, Mr. Russell won academic and law degrees at that institution. After practising law at Oxford, he, following the interim of his political career, entered the real-estate business at Gulfport. He was lieutenant-governor during Mr. Bilbo's first term, and was governor of the state from 1920 to 1924.

During the term of Mr. Russell as governor, the rising tide of democracy in Mississippi began to show grotesque evidences of the irrepressible conflict which it represented. This was the period in which the more advanced sections of the South were making every effort to utilize new economic forces in order to balance the old complete reliance upon a toppling agriculture. Mississippi was not able to fall into step with this general movement because her energies at the moment were being consumed by internal struggles. Violent resentments against all "enemies of the people"—deep jealousies and hatreds, inhibited for years—sprang savagely to the surface and held the stage against constructive programs.

In Mississippi the wave of partly demagogic denunciation of "the interests," which had swept the country a decade or so before, was just then taking form. In the minds of the newly powerful hill people of Mississippi, the large corporations and "trusts" became confused with their old masters, the delta folk. Several strong groups in Governor Russell's legislature were arrayed against the industrial interests. Corporations were vehemently prosecuted under the anti-trust laws. Under a temporary in-junction, all Ford dealers in the state were compelled to cease operations for six weeks. Likewise, all insurance companies, except a few small local organizations, were restrained from selling policies in the state for a certain period; as a result, a number of the larger companies with-drew their agencies.

4

Control of the state schools has been an issue between factions of the Democratic party in Mississippi for at least forty years; it may be said with accuracy that the issue has been a sensitive and pressing one since the term of Governor Russell. If such a situation appears out-landish and almost barbaric to the citizens of other states, one must realize that Mississippi presents, in a highly magnified form, the political jeopardy of all state educa-tional institutions; the scoffer must also bear in mind the fact that state and other public school systems offer one of the most obvious and potentially powerful sources of political organization. That Mississippi happens to have embraced this particular form of political alignment is patently unfortunate for the general cause of education; yet it may be held with some assurance that alignments based upon industrial and religious competitions, such as other states have now and then exhibited, are fraught with quite as much danger to the welfare of the fields represented.

At any rate, among the dismissals supposedly engineered by Governor Russell was that of Henry Whitfield, who had for years been president of the Mississippi State College for Women at Columbus. As head of M.S.C.W., Mr. Whitfield had attempted to make use of a rather remarkable device to unify the conflicting factions of his state. Of the four state colleges in Mississippi, M.S.C.W., with about fifteen hundred students, is the largest. Each county in the state has an established quota of students eligible for the institution. Since the University of Mississippi at Oxford has always maintained a reputation of catering mainly to the delta people, and since the Agricultural and Mechanical College at Starkville is primarily designed to fill the needs of the inhabitants of the hill country, Mr. Whitfield conceived the idea of trying to minimize social strife in the state by creating common interests and sympathies among the women students of all classes who should attend M.S.C.W. Towards this end, exclusive social organizations were never allowed; all students occupied similar quarters in dormitories; and all were required to wear simple uniforms of navy blue suits with black hats.

How conspicuous the colleges have been in the class warfare of Mississippi can be illustrated by two stories well known to people of the state. The A. and M. college has never allowed social fraternities, while the University of Mississippi—"Old Miss"—has always desired to encourage them. During the governorship of Mr. Russell fraternities at the University were abolished. It is generally said that during his college days at the University Mr. Russell had so resented the air of superiority assumed by fraternity members that he, a leader of the non-fraternity element, had taken oath that he would some day become governor of Mississippi and destroy the caste system of his Alma Mater.

There is a second story to the effect that Mr. Russell harbored a deep antipathy against a fellow-student who was supposed to have black-balled young Russell's name when it was presented for membership in one of the organizations. When Mr. Russell reached the governor's chair, so the story goes, this old school enemy of his had become regional representative of one of the large school-book concerns. As his revenge for the college incident, Mr. Russell is said to have removed all this company's books from the Mississippi schools and to have replaced them with the wares of a rival publisher. While these interpretations may be partly the figments of partisan politics, their very currency indicates a trend of thought which is of deep significance.

At the expiration of Mr. Russell's term in 1924, Mr. Whitfield, the deposed president of M.S.C.W., announced for governor to oppose Mr. Bilbo, who then was in a position to return to the capital. The subsequent election of Mr. Whitfield was attributed to the campaign of retribution conducted in his favor by the alumnae of M.S.C.W. and the friends of other school men who had been ousted by Mr. Russell. Upon his accession Governor Whitfield dutifully readjusted the personnel of the educational institutions; he also took pains to reëstablish fraternities and sororities at the University of Mississippi. When Mr. Whitfield died in office, he was succeeded by Lieutenant-Governor Dennis Murphree. In 1928 Mr. Murphree ran for governor against Mr. Bilbo. By this time Mr. Bilbo had reorganized his political machine well enough to win the race, although the fierceness of the Murphree campaign during the ten days prior to the election cut down Mr. Bilbo's majority to a meagre 7,000 votes.

In the summer of 1930, two years after his return to the governor's chair, Mr. Bilbo had gained sufficient control over the school board of trustees to enable him to dismiss and replace 179 officials and faculty members of the four state colleges. He is quoted as having said to the newspaper reporters, "Boys, we have just hung up a new record." The reverberations of horror and official denunciations over the country are well known. The American Medical Association, the Association of Colleges and Secondary Schools of the Southern States, and the American Association of University Professors are among the organizations which disqualified the Mississippi colleges.

Though I venture no defense of Mr. Bilbo, I submit
that his action was humanly understandable. In the light
of precedents clearly established in his state, his onslaught
upon the schools controlled by his enemies was to be expected. Granted that his gesture was climactic in sweep,
one must consider that he had suffered considerable exas-
peration because of his defeat at the hands of Mr. Whitfield and by his narrow escape from the Murphree opposition. Further, it must be held in mind that Mr. Bilbo is a
shrewd politician; that, as such, he had to act in accordance with the peculiarities of his electorate.

5

When Mike Conner became governor of Mississippi
in 1932, it was generally taken for granted that Mr. Bilbo
would seek to follow in the path of the late Mr. Vardaman to the United States Senate. Mr. Bilbo's chance came
in 1934 when he, while retained in Washington by the
Department of Agriculture to clip newspapers at an an-
nual salary of $6,000, heard that Senator Hubert D.
Stephens, of Mississippi, was a member of a committee
which was considering the appointment of Dr. Willard
Thorp to a position in the Department of Commerce.
From that moment Mr. Bilbo's campaign to unseat Mr.
Stephens became the center of interest in Mississippi
politics. Up and down the state Mr. Bilbo went declaim-
ing that his opponent had been in favor of giving a $9,000
job to a "damn Yankee" Republican. At first there were

A familiar silhouette against the southern sky—a gourd pole for martins, with a lard can serving in place of one of the gourds.

Grazing lands in the southern Piedmont.

grave doubts as to whether the college scandal which the former governor had brought upon his state would not make it virtually impossible for him to win the Democratic nomination. Then, there was a good deal of talk about various other scandals, personal and official, with which the name of Bilbo had been connected. But through the blistering days of July and August, the scrawny little man from Poplarville exerted his old-time power at camp meetings, barbecues, county fairs and political "speakings" without number. He promised, among many other items in a platform of twenty-seven points, that he would "redistribute the nation's wealth," starting with immediate full payment of the veterans' bonus. Early in the campaign one of his opponents (not Mr. Stephens) went Mr. Bilbo one better by recommending that the government should simply strike off a couple of million of new bank notes and distribute them until they gave out. Bedecked in his diamond horseshoe pin and frequently in his flaming red necktie, Bilbo countered this proposal by pledging that in Washington he would "make as much noise for the common people as Huey Long, and raise the same kind of hell as President Roosevelt." Also, the state of Jefferson Davis and Pat Harrison heard reverberations of the former governor's celebrated plan for covering Mississippi with paved roads without a penny of cost to the taxpayers. This program involves using the Negro convicts of Mississippi to turn the red-clay hills of the state into brick paving blocks;

when roads constructed of these blocks, according to Mr. Bilbo, become worn on their surface, nothing would be simpler than to have the Negroes turn the bricks over, thereby providing a brand new highway system—still without any cost to the taxpayers. The first Democratic primary cleared the way for the incumbent senator and the former governor. At the run-off primary late in September, Mr. Bilbo, after gaining a sizable majority over Mr. Stephens, was designated as the junior senator from Mississippi. When one of his supporters telegraphed him, "Praise the Lord, you have scourged the money changers from the temple," Mr. Bilbo, a licensed Baptist minister, replied, "Glory, glory, hallelujah!"

If one must seek a classification for the Heflins, Bilbos, and Longs, it would not be too wide of the mark to term them American Fascists (southern style). Their political victories have been won through the mass force of machines built upon every conceivable form of racial, sectional, class, and religious prejudice; these they have been able to fan into furies sufficient to consume their opponents. But, as for actually accomplishing anything to assist their deluded followers, they seem able to operate successfully on the theory that most campaign promises are forgotten between elections. One point, however, must not be overlooked: "the interests," with a few minor exceptions, have not suffered during the ascendancy of these gentry. Perhaps that, after all, is one of the principal reasons why they have been allowed to flourish. "The interests" occasionally might conclude that it is just as well to let the demagogues alone as long as they can keep the people entertained and diverted with funny stories about colored people, and with meaningless thrusts at "menaces" in distant Wall Street or across the Atlantic Ocean.

From all appearances, Tom Heflin has seen his last days as a figure in state or national politics; but his influence lives on in his imitators. It would by no means be discreet for any southerner to venture too many derogatory remarks with reference to Huey Long, for at any moment the Kingfish's *Putsch* in Louisiana may develop in a *coup d'état* involving the entire South, and then all of his subjects who at any time had cast reflections upon him might find themselves in concentration camps for enemies of the people. But one cannot help wondering how the aristocratic folk of the delta lands could ever have permitted the election of Theodore Bilbo as a senator from Mississippi. Possibly they do not consider popular elections worthy of their attention. Indeed, I suspect that if the delta people ever chance to catch an inkling— through the Memphis *Commercial Appeal*—of the current reputation of Mr. Bilbo, they will present to the outside world a stunning revelation of indifference and self-sufficiency.

Chapter VII

Black Figures In the Sun

I

DIVERSE aspects of the color problem in the South, like the spokes of a wheel, revolve about the deeply imbedded notion that the Negro must be kept in his place. Whether this conviction is primarily a hold-over from the elaborate efforts of the latter-day plantation masters and their sycophantic spokesmen to justify slavery on moral grounds, or whether it is mainly the result of the natural jealousy between white workmen and their black competitors, it is the most formidable barrier in the way of an intelligent solution of the racial difficulties in the South. Not only that, but it also at times threatens to vitiate the popular sense of justice and the dignity of the law below the Potomac. One even hears occasionally that there should be two sets of laws in the South, one group for white people and another for Negroes. As a matter of fact, a quite disrespectful person might hint that this double legal standard already exists in effect. Recent efforts, however, to ascertain to what extent the thirteenth, fourteenth, and fifteenth amendments were being observed in the South stimulated two opposite movements in the southern region: one calculated to encourage the

Negro to vote and to serve on juries, and the other designed to "keep the black man in his place."

Just what is this Negro's "place" that we hear so much
about? The other day I went with my small daughter to
a carnival being held on a playground not far from our
home. Standing in front of the ferris wheel, waiting for
a ride, we watched the little cars swinging down from
the sky to the little chugging gasoline motor and then up
towards the stars again. The great turning wheel presented a queer procession of humanity. In one of the cars
sat three college sophomores, trying to keep from showing that they still enjoyed ferris wheels. Then came a
young mill worker and his girl, with hamburger sandwiches in their hands. In the third car, two Negro girls,
their faces powdered and rouged, sat in sedate enjoyment of their afternoon off from nursing duties. As the
next car swung down from its lofty perch, my little com-
panion clutched my hand tighter and gave a short cry
of recognition, for there, with her coal-black escort, sat
the huge bulk of our washerwoman. When the ferris
wheel at last paused and the attendant held back the
safety bar so that we could begin our own ride, we sat
down in a car with three rosy-cheeked neighborhood
children in fluffy dresses of printed muslin in front of us,
and with two overalled farmers, from some hillside cotton patch, behind.

This free mingling of races and classes struck me as

extraordinary; but no one else appeared to be surprised by it. I remembered reading accounts of how the smoldering race hatreds in Chicago in 1919 had been set off into a bonfire of rioting by an incident involving a Negro boy who, while swimming at one of the Chicago beaches, had drifted on a railroad tie across an invisible line into the water reserved for white bathers. I recalled that, in the Alabama town where I live, Negroes and white people, especially on Saturday afternoons, rub shoulders in the crowded grocery stores and butcher shops; and that this town, like many other places in the South, has streets on which white families and Negro people live peaceably on the same block. Later, however, as my young daughter and I waited for Daredevil Danton to climb a hundred feet into the air and dive—"*on* fire *into* fire," as the barker had promised—down into a pool of water with its surface aflame with burning gasoline, I heard a fifteen-year-old girl say, with the unmistakable accent of the hill country, "I don't see how a feller could climb up thar and risk his life in front of a crowd of niggers."

Can it be that this feeling that the Negro has a "place" is a kind of myth in the South; that it is always being forgotten temporarily and then being suddenly remembered, sometimes with violent consequences? Be that as it may, there is no logical explanation of a southern woman's refusal to ride on street cars unless they have separate seats reserved for Negro passengers, while she has left her child at home to be cared for and influenced during its formative years by a Negro nursemaid.

Yet, this conviction that the black man must now and then be intimidated, in order to keep him from forgetting the bounds which southern traditions have set for him, is firmly rooted in the consciousness of many southern people. So unquestioned is this philosophy that at times lynchings are planned and carried through—not under the fierce compulsion of mob hysteria—by men who have calmly resigned themselves to the performance of a painful duty, which, according to their lights, is necessary for the good of society.

My first indirect experience with a lynching took place when I was five years old. On the way to Sunday school, I was rolling a nickel (which was for the collection plate) down a rather steep hill which led from my home to the center of town, where the courthouse was located. Still rolling my nickel along the pavement, I was taking a short cut through the courthouse square when my attention was attracted by a horse and buggy which was disturbing the Sunday morning peace by flying down the street at a very rapid pace. When the horse drew up, panting and frothing, in front of the sheriff's office, I noticed the shoes, and then the legs, of a man dangling from the rear of the buggy. Then several riders came rushing up, descended from their horses, and walked quietly into the courthouse. Soon they came out again, together with several men whom I had often seen about the courthouse, and one of whom I greatly admired because he had once "set me up" to a strawberry ice cream soda at the drugstore. After exchanging a few words among themselves, they took the body of a Negro man from the buggy and carried it into one of the corridors of the building. They tried to open a door; but, apparently finding it locked, laid the body on the floor and stood around waiting for somebody to come and let them in.

All of this excitement had delayed me so much that I suddenly realized that I might be late for Sunday school. It always made you feel funny to have to push your way to your chair while the people were standing up singing. So I rushed off. What was my consternation, however, to discover, just as I was turning the corner by the drugstore, that I had lost my nickel! I ran back to the courthouse. You couldn't go to Sunday school without a nickel! By the time I reached the front of the building I could see that the men had got their door open all right. Everything looked the same as usual. In the bright spring sunshine, several familiar figures were tilted back in their chairs on the stone steps. I must have looked pretty excited, for the man whom I liked the best, the one who had given me the strawberry soda, asked me what on earth was the matter. When I told him, he took me by the hand and walked around with me for several minutes, until we found the nickel. They were singing the first

For the present at least, the problems rising from a concentration of the Negro population lie mainly at the door of the South.

For generations the Negroes were intimately associated with southern families and their customs. They belonged to the established way of life.

song when I got to Sunday school, and Mr. Crenshaw, who owned the store where they sold boys' suits, was playing the violin; but I got in all right, without being seen by anybody very much. . . . At this moment I cannot recall that I heard anybody, then or later, say anything about the lynching.

As well as I can judge at this late date, the whole performance must have been perpetrated in accordance with racial attitudes and theories quite acceptable to the community. The town in which this occurrence took place is one which would most certainly be termed "cultured," with the peculiar connotations which that expression has in the southern mind. If this analysis is valid, one must conclude that the lynching problem in the South involves far more than sporadic eruptions of mob violence occasioned by temporary outbursts of passion. The real menace to legal justice is the tolerance exhibited towards cases of extra-legal procedure in which Negroes are the victims.

2

My second indirect experience with lynching took place one year ago in the Alabama town in which I now reside. I can readily understand how any person who might have come to Tuscaloosa during the late summer and early fall of 1933 would have received an impression of horror. But ordinarily Tuscaloosa is a town of serene

and comfortable beauty, where one may look forward
with happiness to spending the rest of his days. It has
fine old houses, great oak trees, and people whose warm
friendliness makes it easy and agreeable to live with them.
Yet, if Judge Lynch—for even one brief period in fifty-
three years—can hold sway in a town normally as lovely
and charming as Tuscaloosa, what is to be expected from
the prowess of that monster in southern areas less favored
with respect to natural endowments and cultural advantages? (For some records of what Judge Lynch has already accomplished in less favored communities, see
Arthur Raper's *The Tragedy of Lynching*.)

During the spring of 1933, Vaudine Maddox, the
daughter of an itinerant sharecropper, was brutally slain
near Big Sandy Creek in Tuscaloosa County. In due
course of time three Negroes, Dan Pippen, A. T. Harden,
and Elmore (Honey) Clark, were arrested and indicted.
Just what evidence was held against Honey Clark was
not made known to the public; but the consensus among
investigating officials was that Pippen and Harden unquestionably were guilty of the atrocious crime with
which they were charged.

On June 22, as preparations were being made for trying the Maddox case in Tuscaloosa, Judge James E. Horton, in Athens, granted a third trial to Heywood Patter-
son, one of the Scottsboro defendants. His opinion was
a tremendous challenge to that dubious form of southern

chivalry which a few years ago found an appropriate vehicle in the Ku Klux Klan. Referring to Victoria Price
and Ruby Bates, the accusers in the Scottsboro affair,
Judge Horton declared: "History, sacred and profane,
and the common experience of mankind teaches that
women of the character shown in this case are prone for
selfish reasons to make accusations of rape and of insult
upon the slightest provocation, or even without provocation, for ulterior motives."

Even before Irving Schwab and Allan Taub, of New
York, and Frank B. Irvin, of Birmingham, emissaries of
the International Labor Defense, arrived in Tuscaloosa
to defend one of the Negroes in the Maddox case, a
crowd of country boys had gathered at the jail one Saturday night and made an ineffectual demand for the prisoners. But nothing serious had happened. On August 1,
while the sun bore down upon the tin roofs outside and
thickened the air inside the courtroom, the Maddox case
was called. The three Negroes had no lack of counsel to
defend them. Slumping disdainfully under the hard stare
of farmers from the Big Sandy district, the three I.L.D.
lawyers claimed the privilege by reason of a document
purportedly signed by Lucindy Pippen, mother of one
of the prisoners. A rival array of defense attorneys was
composed of two young Alabama lawyers who claimed
that they had been retained by the parents of Pippen.
And a third coterie of defense attorneys consisted of some

of the most capable members of the local bar, who may have been somewhat influenced in their position by the fact that the matter of an adequate defense had carried weight when the Scottsboro case was reviewed by the United States Supreme Court.

Lucindy Pippen forthwith denied that she had ever laid eyes on the document presented by the I.L.D. lawyers. As for the three Negro defendants, their rolling eyes turned with deep gratitude towards the white men who had come there to get them out of that bad trouble. The court then ruled the three out-of-town lawyers to be without jurisdiction and postponed the case indefinitely, on the ground that the jury, which had been present throughout the preliminaries, might have been prejudiced by the conflicts between the defense attorneys.

Meanwhile, several hundred persons had gathered outside the courthouse to mumble to each other about those Communists from the North. It was the kind of crowd which had often gathered in front of those very stone steps on other hot August days to hear Senator Tom Heflin elucidate his theories of white control. They were of the opinion that something ought to be done about those three little Jewish lawyers being paid to spread ideas of social equality among the Alabama Negroes. The circuit judge, mindful of the safety of the visiting lawyers, obtained national guardsmen to escort them to their train. To newspaper reporters he explained at that time, "There is no feeling against the Negroes here, and guards were not needed to protect the defendants."

Two weeks later, on Sunday night, August 13, the sheriff concluded that the tension had reached the breaking point in Tuscaloosa. Three deputies were started off on the road which leads through the hills to Birmingham. On the back seat of the automobile, Pippen, Harden, and Clark were handcuffed. Near the county line half a dozen masked men relieved the deputies of their prisoners. In the lynching which followed, Clark fell to the ground first, wounded by several bullets. Across his form, as he lay half conscious, fell the dead bodies of Pippen and Harden, still handcuffed.

The next day Honey Clark was recaptured. He had crawled to a farmhouse and had lain, trembling with fear and pain, in the barn until his moans awakened a Negro farmer, who called a doctor from town. Returned to jail, Clark signed a statement that he had been unable to recognize any of the men responsible for the lynching. Promptly a special grand jury was set up to investigate the case. So far as the public could gather, the evidence seemed to consist mainly of some bullets said to have been fired at the Negroes. There might have been more bullets for the ballistic experts to examine had it not been for the fact that farmers living near the scene of the lynching had cut some of them into little mementos of the occasion. After several days, the deliberations of the grand jury were interrupted when the attorney-general of Alabama, who had figured prominently in the Scottsboro trials and who had been called to give his personal attention to the Tuscaloosa lynching case, was shot in the heel by a rifle accidentally discharged in a corridor of the courthouse.

While the attorney-general was recovering in a hospital, the guardians of "white supremacy" made an ironic answer to the grand jury by shooting another Negro within a few hundred yards of the fourth tee of the Tuscaloosa Country Club. The second lynching, which occurred on the sixth Sunday after the first one, involved no possible flavor of misdirected Nordic valor, for it happened that the victim was nearly fifty years old, a charity case and a paralytic. The Negro, who had been released under a $300 bond after having been charged with "assaulting" a white woman and running away when she called for help, was taken from his home by six or seven men posing as officers of the law.

The governor of Alabama posted a reward of $400 for the apprehension of those guilty in the second lynching. The Tuscaloosa newspaper printed a ringing first-page editorial entitled "Shall We Accept the Challenge?" Response to this editorial was so favorable that a local "Crusade Against Crime" was almost immediately inaugurated by a Civic Club Committee of Twenty, the executive board of the Tuscaloosa County Federation of

Women's Clubs, the local chapter of the Daughters of
the American Revolution, and the Tuscaloosa Ministerial
Association. Nevertheless, while the crusade was at its
height, the grand jury resumed its deliberations on the
lynching of Pippen and Harden, only to decide within
a few hours that evidence was not sufficient to justify a
bill of indictments. Official investigation of the second
lynching soon thereafter was concluded in a similar
manner.

Although I grant that loyalty to my town, the desire
to defend its reputation, and warm friendship with its
people may color my judgment in this particular, I venture to assert that none of the lynchings would have taken
place had it not been for the resentment directly created
by the three Communist lawyers who deliberately irritated a disturbed situation by their offensive presence.
While my very closeness to the Tuscaloosa tragedies
may render me incapable of giving a completely detached
analysis, it is my opinion that the court officials in the
cases would have apprehended and punished the of-
fenders if it had been possible for them to obtain the
necessary evidence. Again, I am convinced that the "best
people" of the town wished to support the cause of justice. That these considerations should be true, however,
gives an almost unspeakably serious import to the situation. If the occurrence of lynching in the South could be
traced to such a thing as a few cases of corruption in

official circles, the removal of a certain number of individuals could be managed without much difficulty. But
the trouble is far deeper. I am afraid that the popular indifference which was an element in my first experience
with lynching, and which played its part in my second
experience of a like nature, will be the basic offender in
future lynchings untold—unless the "best people" are
willing to be more unrelenting in their demands for a
civilized attitude, and unless they are willing to take personal and commercial risks in making these demands
known. The tragedy of the Tuscaloosa lynchings was
summed up by one of the court officials who told a group
of men that the lynchers would have been apprehended
within twenty-four hours after the commission of their
crime—if public opinion in the county had been un-
flinchingly and aggressively on the side of the law.

3

For the same set of reasons which make it impossible
for the Bourbons and the upper middle classes of the
South to blame the glorification of Huey Long, Theodore Bilbo, and Tom Heflin entirely upon the vagaries
of the "hill billies," "red necks," and "white trash," the
"best people" of the southern states cannot shift moral
responsibility to other shoulders in every case having to
do with mistreatment of the Negro. Their tendency to
do so must be recognized as a bitter social effect of snob-

bery in its most perfidious form. Southerners of a certain type like to imagine that special bonds exist between them and the Negro descendants of the plantation economy. But this bond, it must be admitted, is largely a sentimental one, for it does not always prove to be effective when the Negro needs it most.

When I wore short trousers and was riding on Pullman cars for the first time, my principal interest, aside from the mystery of the seats transformed into beds, was to gauge the treatment accorded me by the porter. I had been previously assured that the porters were always able to tell "nice people" at once. And almost above everything else I desired to be classified in that group. Like so many southern people, we had been deprived for at least one generation of the economic possessions so necessary for outward respectability. Having noted with a certain tacit scorn the appearance of a moneyed class which bore no blood relationship to the plantation group destroyed by the Civil War, we had found ourselves in the hazardous position of maintaining a sense of superiority on the basis of a past which grew increasingly shadowy and uncertain. Also, we had been alarmed to observe that a numerous class of unsuccessful families had begun to trace specious ancestral lines to Carolina plantations ruined by the war. These pretenders were more abhorrent to us than the shrewd newly rich.

In this quandary over our real positions the Negroes

seemed to be the most reliable touchstone. For generations they had been intimately associated with southern families and their customs. They had belonged to the established way of life. As I look back now at that small boy on the Pullman car, I am confident that his wistful discernment would furnish an accurate source picture of the complex texture of racial attitudes in the South.

There were the travelers who sought special attentions through large tips to the porter. They called the black man "George" or "Sam." It was up to him to give them what they paid for. But all his chores for these people were performed with exaggerated deftness and ungenuine courtesy. They had too many pillows, were brushed too often, had more bags for their hats than they could use. These over-attentions pleased the large tippers; they amounted to "service." But such travelers never felt a kind of personal relationship with the porter; a kinship bordering upon that of a family tie; a bond resulting from a common way of life and intertwined experiences. They were not interested in what he would probably do when he left the train, what his wife was named, how many children he had—whether he was happy.

To me, however, going to Washington or Atlanta soon after the turn of the century, the Negro porter was an object of awe and, I am sure, of tenderness. I watched with apprehension to see whether he would recognize friendliness in me. I admired his starched white coat, his

immaculate blue trousers and black shoes; his strength
and agility at pulling down the upper berths and his
dexterity in swiftly tossing mattress, blanket, and sheet
to precisely the right positions. I wondered where he slept
at night and whether he was comfortable; in the dining
car I hoped that the people would not be too hungry to
save some good things for the porter. And I so wanted
him to know that I belonged to the "nice people." What
I desired was not an air of servitude and abasement; it was
rather a sense of companionship, unforced and unembar-
rassed on both sides. My innermost knowledge told me
that he and I were parts of the same civilization. He
would be obliged to make a new way for himself and
his children in a world unalterably fixed by the new
tenets of value; I faced the same problem.

How it warmed me inwardly when the porter showed
by inerrant subtlety that we understood each other. I
could laugh with secret delight when he over-attended
the loud and ponderous men and women who tipped
him with dollar bills. I could admire his reserved strength,
his breeding, when he was addressed with rude sharp-
ness and sometimes cursed. By far the most subtle of all,
though, and by far the most significant and yet difficult
to explain, was the deeply felt contempt which we shared
for the hard-faced and disrespectful white people who
would be sauntering past the Pullman cars as they walked
to and from the day coaches over the crunching cinders

of the way stations. Of such people were the sheriffs, the rural storekeepers, the small farmers, the indigent countrymen who loafed in the towns on Saturday afternoons, and the moonshine distillers. One might read in the papers about their candidates for political office. They were the "taxpayers"; as such, they sought to control the legislatures, the courts, the schools. Their political slogan was "white supremacy," which was somewhat less of a threat to the Negroes than a challenge to the formerly acknowledged rulers of the past régime.

4

Summer before last, wishing to examine a celebrated old Episcopal church, I drove to an historical town in the Alabama black belt. A sign on the church door told me that the key was to be obtained at the home of Jane Jones across the street. Jane Jones, as I should have guessed from the lime scattered about her front yard and the extreme neatness of her small cottage, was an ancient slave woman. The home of white people in corresponding circumstances would probably have been slovenly. But I did not at first realize in the dim light that she was a Negro, and as a consequence I addressed her as "Miss Jones" and took off my hat. Though I almost at once thereafter clapped my hat back on and began to call her "Jane," in approved southern fashion, my initial behavior had touched a complex of emotions in the old woman's mind; it gave me an entrance into her thought which I, as a southern man, could not have gained otherwise.

At the same time pleased and suspicious, she asked me, "Who is you?" Establishing myself as reputable by naming some of the old families once identified with that region, I asked her why all these fine people had moved away. "A new man owns the town," she said. "They sold off all their land because they couldn't work the fields themselves." One by one, she told me where in-dividual members of the old families had sought new paths after the Civil War. Her voice and manner carried an unmistakable accent of aggrieved disappointment, a sense of neglect and desertion. She was telling me a funda-mental truth: that the white planters, unmindful of their obligations, had left the Negroes behind with their com-mon enemies, to shift for themselves against overwhelm-ing odds. At the moment I felt that Jane Jones had leveled a more justifiable criticism against the South than had Harriet Beecher Stowe.

"The colored people go too when they can," she added. "I have a niece in Pittsburgh—principal of a school. The white people are as nice to her as they can be." Then, with a sudden change of manner, she nodded toward the house next door and shrewdly covered her boldness by saying, "The white people that live in that house are nice to me—as nice as you please." But the other direction of feeling was exhibited when she told me of a visit to her nephew in Chicago (she called him her "niece") and of how he had taken her to see his place of employment at a Ford plant. "There was Mr. Henry Ford himself," she continued with a covert gleam; "he was dressed in overalls, working like everybody else—not just standing around in fine clothes bossing the hands. When my niece introduced me to him, he bowed as nice as you please. 'Howdy-do, Miss Jones'—that's what Mr. Henry Ford himself said to me in Chicago."

Half believing this fantastic story, I at the same time knew that Jane Jones neither expected nor wished me to accept it at face value; she did not want me to call her "Miss Jones." She was telling me something profound and true—a story of neglect. Had not the white people, *her* white people, escaped from the desolated farm lands to the cities of the North and the new towns of the South? "I told my white folks not to sell their places and go off," she went on, reading my face. What parallels of experience and philosophy there were between us. . . . "I told them to keep their homes. Sometimes they would come back for visits—the older ones—looking so thin and pale it made me sad. I would watch them going to church, and they would always come by to see me." But pride and spirit supplanted the softer emotion. "The young colored people that have been North say they are going back," she volunteered. "I ask them how they'll get there—'ride a mile and walk ten? Well, go on then,' I tell them. I

want to go to Chicago and Pittsburgh again myself as
soon as there's another excursion."

When I asked her whether the Negroes were happy
in the North, her eyes twinkled with sly triumph inter-
mixed with a play of veiled distrust. Did the white people,
then, leave her this house? "No, sir. My husband built
this house and had other property when he died. See
that filling station on the corner where those white men
are sitting around? I sold them that property. Now and
then the old people send me little presents for taking care
of the church." She opened the screen door and directed
my attention to a large framed lithograph hanging prominently in her front hallway. It represented a famous
American. "I nursed him," explained Jane Jones. "He
gave me the picture."

5

Although the northward migrations of Negroes, so
widely noticed during the World War period, have continued, the pace has been slower during the decade just
past. It is unreasonable for the southern commentator to
evade the issue by insisting too broadly that such migrations now offer an automatic solution of the South's color
problem. One might almost as well await a total absorp-
tion of Negro blood by the white race, for in its own
category racial admixture is as pronounced as emigra-
tion. However much the data may be juggled to suit the

theory of any given observer, the following basic figures remain: of the 11,891,143 Negroes in the United States in 1930, 9,361,577 of them lived in the South. While the white population of the South has almost trebled since 1880, the proportion of Negroes to the total southern population decreased only from 36 to 24.7 per cent from 1880 to 1930. What situations may be revealed in twenty, fifty, or a hundred years are interesting subjects for conjecture. But for the present, at least, the problems rising from a concentration of the Negro population lie mainly at the door of the South.

If the nonassimilation of the Negro represents a problem in the United States as a whole, in which he constitutes approximately one-tenth of the total population, then that problem obviously is greatly intensified in the South, where at present every fourth person is a Negro. Quite aside from such abstract concepts as human freedom and justice, can the South longer afford to jeopardize its economic future by continuing to harbor various delusions which are calculated to keep so large a part of its population in poverty and ignorance? No idealistic philosophy should be required to make the most practical-minded southern business man realize what he is losing in economic productivity and purchasing power because of the South's persistent failure to accept the Negro as a valuable human resource well worth developing.

In the southern states, to be sure, some rays of light

"Pulling" charcoal after it has been smoldering in a sod mound.

"Black figures in the sun"—a Negro tenant farm.

have begun to break through the clouds that have always
obscured realities pertaining to the Negro question. The
South is far from being totally without its intelligent
opinion on the subject. Grover C. Hall, editor of the
Montgomery *Advertiser*, has won a Pulitzer prize for his
courageous fight against the Ku Klux Klan; the Birmingham *News* in 1934 was accorded first honorable mention
in the Pulitzer awards for editorials of the previous year,
in recognition of its vigorous denunciation of the state
of mind which permits lynchings in the South; and the
Tuscaloosa *News*, as I have already said, came forth with
a strong and enlightened editorial policy when the racial
discord was at its height in that town in 1933. Also in
Tuscaloosa, a Baptist minister, without losing any of his
popularity, has been suggesting that a concentration upon
educational advantages for the Negro would be a logical
interest for any persons who might be obsessed by the
belief that the black man is a savage whose presence im-
perils the safety of life in the South. Julian Harris, of the
Atlanta *Constitution*, and George Fort Milton, of the
Chattanooga *News*, are among the southern editors who
have been notably active in efforts to bring about a new
deal for the Negroes.

In spite of these and many other favorable signs, however, there is much evidence that such bright flares of
enlightenment frequently serve only to throw into contrast a melancholy background of frustration and defeat.

Even in Atlanta, where it was organized in 1920 under the directorship of Dr. M. Ashby Jones, then pastor of the Ponce De Leon Baptist Church, the Commission on Interracial Coöperation has been forced to deal with a considerable amount of antagonism. Yet, the realization that the dark patterns of this background of imbedded traditionalism will absorb and nullify all but the most inflexible rays of light should spur imaginative southerners on to more consecrated efforts. Neither ignorance nor despair should be allowed to "keep the Negro in his place."

Since I can lay no claims to profound scholarship in the fields of history or sociology, my impressions with respect to the Negro problem—as well as my notations pertaining to other matters relating to southern life—are the reactions produced by sounds and images registered over a long period of years in a mind which, for all its faults, is of the South and southern. As an Alabamian, and as one not without an intuitive bias on the side of traditionalism and the *status quo*, I am often conscious of being compelled literally to think twice about issues in which the Negro is concerned. First, upon hearing adverse criticisms of conditions as they are, I feel a resentment and an impulse to defend my state and my people; but then I have to ask myself whether a deeper loyalty does not place me under a compulsion to wrestle with these disagreeable challenges until the truth which they contain has been separated from what is false or merely sensational about them. I wonder whether this is not the sort of thing that is taking place in the minds of many other southerners today.

For the sake of the future of the South as a whole, we must in some way make it possible for the Negro to discharge the obligations of dignified citizenship to the limit of his abilities. Before we can enter effectively upon a program designed to establish the black man in this new "place," we shall have to go through the painful process of transferring our present forced reasoning into the more agreeable realm of intuitive acceptance.

Chapter VIII
The Machine's Last Frontier

I

HALTED by the depression in their program of industrial expansion, the southern states today hang undecided between farm and factory. Naturally the present retardation of manufacturing has stimulated movements back to the land in all sections of America. But the South is the last frontier of the industrial revolution in this country. As a consequence, the machine had not been thoroughly integrated into its economic life before the depression came. Mill workers still talked the language and carried mental images of the farm. They had not made up their minds whether it was better for them to grow or to weave those snowy cotton fibers with which their lives seemed so inextricably bound.

Home in the hills for Sunday, workers in the new steel mills would compare their experiences with those of their brothers who had remained true to agriculture. Migratory lines of transient workers moved in country denim overalls from mill to mill in a more or less tentative and investigative spirit. Sometimes they would become settled in a factory town, living with a sense of permanence and security in one of the company houses; sometimes they preferred the independence of the small farm and would return there to be content with a somewhat reduced monetary income. Such has been the picture in the industrial laboratory of the South during the past ten years.

Now that a distinct setback has been suffered in the development of industry, factory wages have become more nearly equalized with the income of a small farmer, the effects of the NRA and those of the AAA having more or less balanced each other in the matter of increased incomes which they have given to the industrial workers and the independent farmers. The problem now resolves itself into the question of choosing between two ways of life. Shall they stick it out in the factory or turn back to the land? The delicately balanced alternatives faced by the wage-earners at this moment in the South are also being weighed in the minds of the entrepreneurs. Shall they return to the cultivation of cotton, tobacco, sugar cane, and rice under a system of agriculture largely manual, or shall they continue their efforts to carry these raw products farther along the economic progression by maintaining their faith in the machine?

On the one hand, the indigenous bias of the southerner tends to influence him toward a sole dependence upon the soil. Characteristically he lacks the natural feeling for the machine which marks so much of the artisan population of the middle western states. That impetus to factory development contributed by the industrially skillful German immigrants has been lacking in the South. Men from the gulf states do not make very successful automobile mechanics. Few southern men tinker with electrical contrivances or chisel and plane pieces of wood into curious shapes in their basements as a hobby; they prefer to breed dogs or to cultivate roses in their hours of relaxation.

While it is true that many Scotch-Irish and German families have settled among the English inhabitants of the Piedmont regions of the Carolinas and Georgia, the hill people continue to take pride in their Anglo-Saxon ancestry. The southern population, with its deeply ingrained economic philosophy, plants itself as a bulwark against change. Italians brought a few years ago to Louisiana to grow strawberries were viewed with the utmost suspicion by the natives. When a progressive organization recently imported several German families in the hope that they would demonstrate the possibilities of intensive farming on the river lands of Georgia, the newcomers were quite unable to enlist the interest of their neighbors. Nevertheless it is true that the most profitable cultivation of cotton in Alabama is at present being carried on in a county far removed from the old black belt and almost entirely inhabited by Germans of a previous migration.

Many natives of the South have never seen a Scandinavian or a Russian. People from Georgia travel a considerable distance to wonder at the habits and hear the language in a settlement of Greek sponge fishers on the west coast of Florida. While the Spanish influence is conspicuous in other parts of Florida, the distinctly French savor of Louisiana makes this latter region the only strictly southern state which has not inherited its social and economic points of view almost solely from seventeenth- and eighteenth-century England.

2

Southerners familiar with the developing iron and steel districts of the South during the last fifteen years have observed ample evidence of the lack of industrial predisposition among the natives. Iron furnaces periodically would be blown in and then abandoned for no apparent cause. Managements would shift. Northern capitalists would lend their support temporarily. On occasion even Japanese industrialists took a hand. For a time the great crimson glow of the "runs" of molten iron glorified the night skies for miles around the active furnaces; then a lull in work ensued, the skies became dark except for moon and stars, and tough-fibered grass again sprang up in the sand where the hot metal had been poured into "pig" iron. Steel ladders leading to the lofty retort towers would rust in the humid air, and under the beating sun the paint would crack and crinkle on the roofs of the deserted buildings. White and Negro laborers would already have gained employment in other furnaces which happened to be in operation near by; or else they would have returned to the land from which they had only recently departed.

Mining of the ferrous ore was pursued in a haphazard fashion. Easily accessible deposits near the surface were ferreted out with picks and shovels, but the red earth was not systematically excavated by efficient methods. Ore washing was accomplished, not by liquid under high pressure, but as a rule only by water conducted over the metal from a limited height. As a result of wasteful methods allowed in some of the pipe factories fifteen years ago, the surrounding earth became packed with oddly-shaped metal which had overflowed from the carelessly filled molds and had then been pitched from the windows. Later the salvaging of this discarded iron brought many thousands of dollars to the more efficient operators of these plants. In the southern coal mines the most visible parts of the rich veins could be tapped without the aid of machinery; as a result, the coal business in the South for many years was little more than a dabbling variation of the agricultural economy. Not a true industry, it was simply another way of gaining a livelihood by digging in the ground with hand tools.

On the other hand, the comparative backwardness of farming in the southern states has been greatly emphasized during the past ten years. While the harvesting machine has roared through many a grain field in parts of Texas, Kentucky, and Tennessee, the crops most identi-

Workers' houses near a small iron furnace.

River-bottom land annually devoted to cotton or corn for a hundred years.

fied with the southern region are still gathered mostly by hand. The advantages incident to machine agriculture have not been available in the South to any appreciable extent. The vast cacophony of motor-driven plows has not yet ravaged the far-spreading peace of the Shenandoah Valley. Even so, the South has suffered frequently from an over-production of cotton. A further hindrance to agricultural profits below the Potomac, of course, has been the tenant system of farming, that clumsy survival of slavery.

Although the rich cotton lands were able to compete successfully with the rocky New England farms during the earliest years of the United States, the introduction of machines and technical skill in the North soon gave a different color to the scene. The North began to hustle—but the South cherished its social stratification and fell into economic stagnation. The very ease with which a crop might be produced in the South became a boomerang to the region.

In view of these conditions, it was not surprising that the tenant farmers and the poverty-stricken people of the hills should have beaten a wide track to the southern cotton mills at their first opportunity. Wages of $10 a week in the factories meant unaccustomed luxury to folk whose former income often had been no more than $10 a month in actual money. Again, they found that the mills freed them from onerous competition with Negro tenant farmers. To them as a rule was entrusted the simple task of tending spindles; later they might hope for the more advanced job of threading bobbins for the weaving machines. Occasionally the men became mechanics or foremen. Even positions as superintendents might reward ambition and reliability demonstrated over a period of years. But the most complicated techniques, such as dyeing thread and designing patterns for the cloth, very frequently had to be reserved for skilled workmen from one of the industrialized countries of Europe. Consequently, the cotton mills ushered a number of Swiss and Slovakian technicians into the southern factory towns, just as the steel and iron factories imported German and English experts to carry out the specialized processes of their plants. Inexperience on the part of the native southerner soon made itself felt as a discouraging handicap to advancement in the mills. Hard physical work, however, like sweeping the mill floors and cleaning the windows, was given to Negro women, while the Negro men shoveled coal in the boiler rooms and trucked the heavy bales of cotton.

3

Child labor in the new southern mills did not perpetuate the barbaric system associated with the earlier day in New England, for by the time the cotton industry moved southward machines of marvelous abilities had absorbed the tasks formerly relegated to children. The sons and daughters of the mill hands frequently attended school in factory town, a privilege which many of them would not have enjoyed in their rural homes. Furthermore, the children generally ate more wholesome food in the mill villages than had been offered them in their cabins on the farm or hillside. Instead of an unvaried diet of corn meal, "white meat," and turnip greens, many of the factory towns afforded large quantities of excellent milk from the company dairies, a number of vegetables, various kinds of wheat bread, chickens, and beef from the company farms, as well as fruits and eggs. Respite from hookworm and malaria was in itself a boon of inestimable value. By means of games, musical and dramatic clubs, and church assemblies, the socialization of these formerly isolated rural people often was decidedly advanced. Here the children sometimes heard about Jack and his beanstalk and Little Tom Tucker, whom they possibly might never have known in their hillside cabins. They bedecked themselves in gossamer fairy wings and stiffly precise dresses of gay colors to dance and sing through such juvenile triumphs as "Hop-O-My-Thumb" and "Rose Red and Lily White."

On gala occasions the five-year-olds, with sparkling eyes and twinkling legs, might prance about a tinseled stage singing with their own pronunciations,

> "We're elfs, we're elfs;
> We play with ourselfs."

One who had seen the colorless cheeks and thin bodies of children of the same age on southern tenant farms could but find himself happily moved by such a spectacle. Moreover, the mothers of the young actors frequently were taught by experts such useful techniques as dressmaking and household management. Through adult education the men often learned to read and write their own names for the first time.

Not all the mills, to be sure, provided such admirable social conditions for their employees. The exigencies of competitive industry sometimes allowed the workers only the barest necessities of life. For everything was not always roseate for the factory owners and the bankers who supplied their capital. Sometimes, as at Gastonia and Marion, the owners were compelled to drive their workers hard to keep their own heads above the rising tide of competition. Conditions were mixed in the partially industrialized South of the 1920's.

It must be emphasized that neither the employees nor the managerial classes in the South had become habituated to the industrial revolution when the depression arrived. The machine was on the frontier: it had neither been turned back nor assimilated. Through that strange underground system of communication, by means of which people of similar minds exchange information, word even now continues to pass from mill to mill and from farm to farm among members of the working fraternity. It

may be that such and such a factory is soon to increase
or deplete its number of employees. The rumor is carried at once through the countryside by that mysterious
interchange of whispers. Similarly in previous years the
tenant farmers had been able to disseminate among themselves news of agricultural prosperity or prospective failure on the various plantations. Factory managers in the
South often explain, "We do not need labor agents. The
working people for miles around know what is going
on in all the mills."

Those rural cabins this year again occupied may have
been closely guarded by neighbors who remained behind
while the adventurous made a sortie into factory town.
Yet, on the paved highways of the South just now it is
not uncommon to see a man and wife with their brood
of children trudging along under the scorching sun, or
sitting with their small bundle of possessions on a red-
clay embankment under a tree. Come what may, they
move vagrantly down the road. In a day or perhaps five
days they will sojourn for a period, possibly at a tenant
hut in the fields or mayhap at a company house near a
cotton mill.

Somewhat different in character from the tenant farmers and the hill people are the mountaineers of the Carolinas and Tennessee who have also experimented with
machine civilization in the South during the last ten years.
From the very windows of many of the new mills, as at

Gastonia in the foothills of the Appalachians, trees on the ridges of the Great Smokies or the Blue Ridge Mountains are visible. In general, the mountaineers were the last class drawn upon by the southern factories. Always somewhat disdainful of the "furriners" and "quare critters" of the lowlands, they have not found it so difficult to return to their highland fastness now that employment has waned in the mills. Instead of weaving gingham on the throbbing factory machines, the women have returned to the handicraft production of hooked rugs, homespun cloth, and tufted bedspreads, while the men are again wandering the valleys in search of game or preparing to set their traps to catch fur-bearing animals. Meanwhile they tend their slanting patches of corn, turnips, and sorghum.

Looking narrowly upon the mutations in the flat lands below, they have struck their fiddle strings with hollow reeds and, like the ballad singers of old England and Scotland, have composed their rude verses of detached comment upon the sinking of the Titanic, the death of Floyd Collins, and strikes in the cotton mills. They are able to view the crossed economic tendencies in the South with a certain grave and unbending objectivity. Such novels as Maristan Chapman's *The Happy Mountain* accurately portray the periodic journeys of these people into the centers of modern civilization, and their casual return home at will. But the mountaineers constitute the only definitive class in the South which has been able to maintain a semblance of physical and intellectual detachment from the conflict between industrialism and agrarianism.

The sweep of the factory into the southern states has many aspects which are remindful of the industrialization of Russia. In the first place, the zeal of the movement in the South during the 1920's was comparable to the Russian ardor for a machine economy. Again, the inherent absence of technical skill in the make-up of the southern population is analogous to the Russian situation. If the Soviet plan should fail, it would be interesting to observe the directions taken by the workers now industrially employed. Should the Russians suddenly be caught in a stalled program of economic change, it seems logical to suppose that they would find themselves in a state of uncertainty as between the machine and the farm. That is exactly what has taken place in the South under similar conditions.

4

Midway between the industrial age and the agricultural era, the old-fashioned southern grist mill is symbolical of the present undecided balance between the two economic phases. These single-roomed water-power enterprises for grinding corn into meal have long served as picturesque landmarks on the winding courses of small streams in the South. Some of the older ones are covered halfway up their stone sides with dark green moss; they appear to be veritable boulders with thin sheets of water falling into swirls of foam at their feet. Inside the mill itself one is scarcely able to hear the noise of the water wheel and the grinding stones; the steady beating of the water over the falls dominates all other sounds.

Here no intrusion of machinery disagreeably breaks the charm of the countryside. No whistles, no bells, no smoke, no clattering engines disturb the air. Red birds flash a crimson line from the mossy roof to the gray window sill, and white ducks swim in the mill pond among the water lilies. The miller himself is capital and labor both in one. Mindful of the rights of labor, he sometimes reclines a full long summer afternoon in the languid sunshine on the thick soft grass above the dam, while the splashing waters lull him far from the bins of corn waiting to be shelled and ground within his factory. But solicitous too on the employer's side, he maintains a production curve high enough to care for his trade in the area surrounding his plant. Except for a few months in the autumn harvest season, no modified stretch-out system is ever necessary to meet competition, for mills can be constructed only at certain favorable places, and the water can leap only a limited number of dams in the course of a score of miles. At times, moreover, during highwater intervals and quite frequently during the dry summer months, operations must be curtailed to a certain

At the curb markets are found little bundles of fragrant sassafras, mustard greens flecked with drops of water, butter beans of pale green, prickly okra, buttermilk in green fruit jars, delicate petunias, golden honey.

Saturday morning at the curb market. The women forget business to talk about flowers. The venders inquire of each other about conditions in the cotton and steel mills.

extent by all the mills of that type. Nature's own law of
supply and demand here remains in force.

Perhaps as a result of his attachment to such scenes, the
southerner to this day professes a strong bias in favor of
water-ground meal. Pushed for a scientific explanation
of his prejudice, he will contend that the slowly revolv-
ing stones of the water mills do not become so heated as
to spoil the rich flavor of the grain as it is being ground.
In the larger factories the stones revolve upon each other
at great speed in order to obtain volume production. Steel
grinding, the southerner feels, is the last word in perversity. Be the difference in flavor real or fancied, the southerner's decided views on the subject may be offered as
an assertion of a surviving prejudice against the speed and
volume characteristics of the machine.

On the banks of creeks throughout the South a traveler
this summer can see water-driven grist mills, even during
the low-water periods of the dry season, in operation for
the first time in several years. Once more the miller is
grinding his neighbors' corn into meal and being paid for
his work by retaining a stipulated share of the gross
weight. Old deserted mills have been patiently recon-
structed with rough boards and sheets of galvanized iron
to meet the needs of a return to activity. Representing
an eccentric compromise between the old and the new
régimes, a few single-roomed new mills built of rude tim-
ber are sheltering antiquated grindstones now propelled,

not by water, but by humming little electric dynamos or puffing gasoline motors.

In the surrounding country turnips and sweet potatoes are being grown this year on strips of ground which previously had lain fallow for several planting seasons. Sugar cane has pushed its green shoots through earth not long since deserted for the factory. The tender vines of field peas have begun to climb on freshly cut hickory stakes. So long as there are yams, sorghum, meal, and turnip greens, the people who grow them are measurably able to forget the trail to the factory town. And given in addition a few chunks of smoked ham and bacon from the pigs fattening on acorns and peanuts, they may even come to think of their fortune as being considerably more desirable than that of the mill hands. Withal, they are at home again.

At the same time, their link with urbanization and the machine has not been severed entirely. They persist in retaining a connection with the outside world. Indicating a temporary vacillation, many of them have reverted to the midway handicraft stage. In the hilly sections of Georgia, Alabama, Tennessee, and the Carolinas the number of handicraft products offered for sale in small communities and along the highways has visibly increased during the past two years. Among the items being made in larger quantities and marketed with a fair degree of success are hand-made pottery jars and bowls, pine and

oak chairs with ladder backs and woven textile or cane
seats, fragrant balsam-fir and pine-needle pillows, hooked
rugs and mats, hand-loomed cloth of wool and cotton
mixtures, crudely artistic statuettes fashioned from wood
or clay, miscellaneous boxes and cabinets of split wood
of different colors and highly polished with beeswax, and
many varieties of the quaint embroidery characteristic of
the hill folk. Much of this work represents the old-
fashioned utilization of time and energy but a short while
released from machine-tending at the retarded factories.

Together with these handicraft pieces, products of the
farm in increased quantities are offered for sale by country venders at newly established curb markets in many
southern towns, as well as along the principal highways.
These frequently exhibit significant intermixtures between items of the soil and those associated with the
machine. Little bundles of fragrant sassafras are tied with
narrow strips of checked gingham cloth, eggs are packed
for safety in the hulls of cotton seed, mustard greens
flecked with drops of water fill the recesses of galvanized-
iron washtubs, butter beans of pale green are poured
bountifully into brown shoe-cartons from mail-order
houses, prickly okra is spread upon cotton sheets lying
on the ground, buttermilk is abundantly displayed in
green fruit-jars, delicate petunias nod their heads above
the wide mouths of pickle bottles, and brilliant carnations
adorn the shining rims of tin lard-buckets. Behind an

infinitely complicated set of scales, in which he evidently takes much pride, a grizzled patriarch of the hills may offer golden honey for sale in quart milk-bottles, which do not have to be weighed.

Regardless of the unwavering sun, the mid-summer flowers spread an aureole of color above the onions, potatoes, and string beans at their feet. The burnt-almond wild butterfly (or rose-in-the-woods), blue forget-me-nots, tall hollyhocks, long-petaled daisies, varicolored phlox, sweet peas, luxuriant hydrangeas, sun-like marigolds, zinnias, gladioli, snapdragons, corn-flowers, cosmos, larkspur, crimson and white roses, cape jessamines, lady fingers, crepe myrtle, and ragged robins blend their hues. The women forget business to talk about the flowers. One says that the colors of the hydrangea can be determined by laying either blueing or rusty nails by the roots of the plant. Another tells that she ob-tained the seed for her "fever-few" blossoms, or summer chrysanthemums, from a mail-order house in a distant city. A sun-baked farmer slyly takes his leave from a table of ribbon-cane syrup to obtain the luxury of a "boughten" shave at a hotel barber shop.

At the curb markets and at their roadside stands the venders inquire of each other about conditions in the cotton and steel mills. This plant is going to shut down; that one is about to take on a few more hands. They complain because too many are trying to farm: agriculture cannot support everybody; with cotton so low, nobody can make anything by growing that. There is a whispered rumor about work in a kraft paper mill; whereupon the farmers desert the tables where their wares are displayed and gather into small knots to exchange confidences and advice about new jobs in the factories. Suspended halfway between industry and agriculture, these people are ready at a moment's notice to swing in either direction. They broadly represent the southern attitude at this time. For the industrial revolution has neither been defeated nor accepted in the South. On the frontier it awaits a turn of circumstances.

Chapter IX
They Are Not All Monsters

I

TALLADEGA Creek must rise somewhere in the green foot-hills of the Appalachians in northeast Alabama. Even-tually its clear waters merge with the muddy Coosa River; just where I cannot say. Nor should I care to post myself by observation of this matter of small geography. It is not pleasant to watch sparkling streams lose them-selves in the nameless heterogeneity of great muddy rivers. In my boyhood I only knew that we seemed to come suddenly upon Talladega Creek after driving about three miles in almost any direction from the town where we lived in the domain of a mountain so ominously formed that we called it the Sleeping Giant.

Anywhere we went driving it appeared that sooner or later the horses' hoofs all at once would begin to clatter over the boards of a covered bridge spanning Talladega Creek, or else the horses would stand knee deep in the cool waters of the ford. The sun through overhanging leaves dappled the bright waters, spiders skimmed reck-lessly on their long thread-like legs, and always there were gossamer-winged tiny elfin creatures of the stream, perhaps to see that the horses did no harm. All katydids and tree frogs must have known the fords as lovely places and gathered there to blend their musical notes. Possibly they sang, as a cat purs, with a kind of reflex emanation into pervasive serenity. And as we emerged with water dripping from the legs of the horses and from the shining spokes and tires of the phaëton, it seemed always that we were in sight of the majestic Sleeping Giant.

Early in our high school careers, however, Chocolocca Creek—which was ten miles from town—began to supplant the nearer stream in the affections of my confrères. Even before we had access to automobiles we preferred outings at Jackson Shoals on the more distant creek. For on Chocolocca a power company had built a large hydroelectric generating plant. After emphasizing the fact that we had been far from insensible to the natural charms of Talladega Creek, I trust that I may be held guilty of no unnatural predilections when I frankly confess that we soon became overwhelmingly more interested in the mystery of the dynamos and transformers at Jackson Shoals.

My present feeling is that we at that age were philistines because we had not then come into full inheritance of the traditional attitudes and literature bearing upon the supposed harmony between nature and a good man. Again, we lived quite unaware of the past and present agonies of mankind in his adjustments to what is called the industrial revolution. Beyond our ken was the enormous difficulty of humanity, having once brought itself partially into a state of docility before unfriendly natural elements, in so soon being faced by the necessity of making new adjustments with elements half natural and half the result of man's own ingenuity. Being ignorant of the history of the machine since James Watt, we had no reason to look narrowly upon the flashing wires and humming coils at Jackson Shoals. If we could not then comprehend the physical suffering which the machine was capable of bringing to man, far less could we envision the long course of intellectual and emotional alterations in established mental attitudes which would have to be accomplished before "educated" humanity could accept the machine without bias. We did not know that the currents and backgrounds of literature and philosophy would have to absorb a new coloration before their votaries could be happy in the world of the dynamo. Therefore, without benefit of Stuart Chase, Eugene O'Neill, Irving Babbitt, and Paul Elmer More, it was our experience to be there admiring the hydro-electric plant, instead of at one of the traditionally acceptable moss-covered water mills in a sylvan glade of Talladega Creek. . . . Such reflections as these have led me to wonder whether a normal person, if left to a self-expression uninfluenced by traditional images of literature and philosophy, would actually feel the kind of aversion to the machine which has been professed by persons who claim to see in industrialization only the final damnation of the human race.

During my boyhood, however, my associates and I did not find ourselves attracted by the cotton mills. On the contrary, there was something abhorrent about them. We knew the shabby streets, or rather the rutty clay roads, where the factory people lived—two or three families of them in a house that looked forlorn and miserable with its rough unpainted boards and bare yard marked with lines the water had made after splashing from the roof. On Saturday afternoons we would see the mill people, off a few hours from their work. Walking usually in single file, as if they were still following a narrow path over hills in the country, they could be seen going to town. Their shoulders and arms drooped with obvious weariness; soiled lint from the mills hung on their clothing and in their hair. They walked along in single file without talking to each other, about three paces apart, going to town on Saturday afternoon. Now and then we would encounter them in some of the grocery stores. Mainly they seemed to buy snuff and stick candy, but the clerks never paid much attention to them one way or the other. They were just the cotton mill people. The clerks often asked them to wait while other customers were being attended to, and the cotton mill people never seemed to mind.

Now and then, as we were coming home late at night from 'possum hunting, we would see flickering lights in the windows of houses in mill town. Some of those familiar figures—just the same when the stars were overhead as when the night was black and cold—would be walking silently in single file towards the mills, and another line of them would be moving, perhaps even more silently and slowly, towards the places where they were to sleep, and then have breakfast, and then go to work again. Once, while passing through mill town late at night, we heard a high-pitched organ playing a religious tune that we ourselves had heard in Sunday school, and a woman's shrill voice was singing the words. Far off somewhere a lone dog was howling. The kerosene lamps were burning in the windows of some of the houses; the two lines of people were marching again—changing shifts at the mills. "The mill people are all crazy," one of my companions said. "Why?" I asked. "Because they wouldn't live that way if they weren't," he said. And we shrugged our shoulders and kept on our way to our homes. There was one mill girl that we did know actually by name. She was a schoolmate of ours. Although she was about fifteen years old, she was in the first grade, and she could not learn to read. All the other first-graders made fun of her. We heard that she could not learn to work in the mills; so they had sent her to school.

All of that was nearly twenty-five years ago. Today, Talladega Creek is as beautiful and serene as ever. The katydids and the tree frogs still sing there; the great bulk of the Sleeping Giant can still be seen in the distance. The dynamos still hum at Jackson Shoals, but most of the electricity used in the town now comes from huge new plants located elsewhere in the state. As for the pitiful houses of the mill workers, which used to make us shudder, they no longer exist. They have been replaced with neat homes painted white or green; they have gas stoves, electric lights, running water, curtains at the windows, rugs on the floor, and radios. The cotton mill people no longer have lint on their clothing, nor do they seem to walk in single file on their way to town or to their work. Children no longer stand guard at the spindles; it is the regular thing for them to go to school.

Civilization, with the aid of the machine age, has brought such changes to many of the mill workers in the South. Yet, it cannot be denied that many other mill people are still being forced to exist under the horrid conditions of a barbaric past. In the face of these wide differences it must be realized that it is the use which mankind makes of the machines—rather than the machine as such—which determines whether it shall be a blessing or a curse in the South, and elsewhere in the world.

2

Although the problems involving the machine in the South, as witnessed by the recent textile strike, are many and grave, no competent artist would ever paint the picture of southern industry at the present time entirely in somber colors. Bright spots must appear on the canvas, and it is true that the brush occasionally ought to be dipped in phosphorescent paint. Secretary Frances Perkins herself, during a trip to the South in the summer of 1934, declared that her personal inspection of some of the southern cotton mills had demonstrated to her satisfaction that much could be said in praise of them. Since I happen to have some personal knowledge of conditions in the chain of factories upon which Miss Perkins passed a favorable judgment, I count it my privilege to advance some remarks with reference to Cousin Charley's mill.

I must state promptly that the figure I shall refer to as Cousin Charley is not really my cousin at all. He is not merely a single person. A composite of four individuals of the same family, he is none the less a substantial entity. While the persons from whom he is formulated may have rather different complexions, hobbies, places of residence, and tastes in salad dressing, they are all the same at heart. Cousin Charley is a cotton mill owner. He might even be called a magnate. In fact, he owns more mills than anybody else in one of the most industrialized of the southern states, and that fact alone establishes him as not

unworthy of serious biography in this untutored day of
yardstick evaluations.

Yet, Cousin Charley's claim to renown does not rest
mainly upon the triumphant upward surges of the profit
curve on his business graphs. It is not to be expressed in
index figures. Upon the walls of his office there are no
framed proofs of his glory in terms of red and black lines
jogging crazily over purple and green backgrounds; no
ebony monuments celebrate the extent of his acquisitions
for each year since 1897; the decent amenities there are
not at once suppressed by regal manifestoes such as "What
Are The Facts?" and "Time Is Money." Instead, on the
walls of Cousin Charley's office hangs a picture of his
father. The strong gray eyes, the well defined nose and
chin, and the smooth wide forehead have been preserved
in life by Cousin Charley. A visitor to the office is invited
to sit comfortably in a soft rocking chair; if the visitor is
an old friend, he may put his feet on the broad mahogany
desk.

Reading of William Gregg and his Graniteville in the
South Carolina of the 1850's, one cannot escape the suspicion that this "factory master of the Old South" possessed a social philosophy which but faintly perfumed
an avid talent for personal aggrandizement. On occasion
he protested with an almost puritan sanctimony against
the Charleston ordinance that prohibited the use of steam
engines in that city. As a factory master of the modern

South, Cousin Charley has not turned his spindles unprofitably. Yet there are two important respects in which he differs from William Gregg. His immediate family had been accustomed to a fairly satisfactory amount of wealth for several generations. Money produced no sudden hysteria in him; he had seen it before. It had been assimilated into the pattern of his life. He was no Chicago real-estate dealer thrown into frenzied ecstasy at the prospect of a two-car garage and a man servant in brass buttons. Cousin Charley is what might be called a Bourbon in a mild and unassuming way. In the second place, he is to the marrow a native of the state in which his industries have been developed. He knows its black cotton lands, its cool beaches along the Gulf of Mexico, its red iron earth toward the north, and its statuesque pines reaching for the banks of shining clouds afloat in the infinitely blue skies of summer.

When high political office signified the confidence of reputable citizens, rather than a kind of medicine-show shrewdness in barnstorming the backwoods, Cousin Charley's father was governor. It was he who set up a cotton mill on the outskirts of a coal and iron center which was to become the largest city in the state. In 1897 this cotton factory was begun as a civic enterprise to give employment to the hundreds of surplus workers who were flocking in from tenant farm and hillside to seek a better life in the mines and blast furnaces. Under the governor's leadership, members of his family shifted their interests from black belt plantations to factory towns; but their essential characteristics did not change. Cousin Charley therefore inherited spindles instead of furrows; white mill hands instead of Negro farm laborers; instead of concluding his interest in cotton after it had been carried from seed to bale, he found himself under the necessity of attacking a new set of decidedly more complex and unfamiliar processes. At the mills he broke the steel girdles on the bales in order to send the flaky white fibers into contact with the machine.

The problems which he faced taxed Cousin Charley's ingenuity from the outset. Lack of machine consciousness in the South, the absence of technically skilled workmen, bewilderingly complicated systems of banking and accounting, scarcity of capital funds in the South, the stiff competition with established mills in Massachusetts and Connecticut, inadequate railroad transportation and lack of facilities for export from southern ports, the absence of an experienced marketing organization—all these vexed Cousin Charley. He suffered from all the obstacles that beset the other native captains of southern industry so aptly described by Claudius Murchison in *The Virginia Quarterly Review*. Yet he not only survived but also was able to expand his interests until ten or twelve successful mills in various parts of the state came to be under his management. It was not necessary for all the members of the governor's family to flee from the decreasing agricultural profits in the overworked black belt. Mills were procured or built near the old plantation sites, and members of the family, like Cousin Charley himself, gradually transferred their business activities from the soil to the machine.

3

It is possible for a well conducted cotton factory to engage the emotions in such a way as to produce an impression of beauty. As the compressed fibers are released from the hoops and webbing of the bales, they are carried through carding machines which transform the tangled mass into soft and orderly rolls of fleecy white. From this stage the fibers are lightly twisted into strands which are gently folded upon each other in tall containers. Almost vaporous and ethereal in their snowy whiteness, the delicate strands are further blended and then twisted more tightly until they approach the thinness of a pipe cleaner. At this stage they are ready to be spun into thread of solid textile strength.

Looking a hundred yards down a lane of spindles, one is conscious of an orderliness and harmony among the thousands of pieces of diverse mechanism which are so closely synchronized. The identification of harmony with beauty so forcefully revealed by George Santayana rises tentatively to the mind; and the apparent absurdity

Gathering sedge grass for brooms.

A handicraftsman with a foot lathe.

of thinking of Santayana in connection with machinery proves insufficient to cause a total rejection of the idea that a cotton mill possesses its aesthetic values. The noise which the spindles produce is not a clatter; rather than being a cacophony of many dissimilar vibrations, it seems to have a sustained pitch and a tone quality as of the whirring of many wings in unison.

No startling metallic crashes break upon the steady hum of the spindles; they neither scream nor roar. Above the spinning frames on tracks suspended from the ceiling move the "cleaners" in a slow and graceful rhythm. Years ago, as I have said, cotton mill people walking the streets on Saturday afternoons could always be distinguished by the dingy lint hanging from their clothing and hair; but now the "cleaners," gliding with their uncanny precision over the spindles, blow the vagrant lint to the floor, where it can easily be swept up. Operatives no longer carry lint on their clothing; in their neat blue uniforms they stand in the aisles, their agile fingers ready to mend broken threads and to remove filled spindles. With the constantly improved machinery, there is less and less for them to do.

In the darksome past of the cotton industry, children used to wind the light thread into heavier yarns to suit the requirements of the market. Now that operation is performed by machines of almost unbelievable dexterity. Child labor has never been a problem in Cousin Charley's mill; there always have been too many destitute adult farmers who have been ready enough to undertake whatever work might be available. Since the introduction of machines capable of replacing fifty or more operatives, there has been no reason for child labor in any of the cotton mills. Even the New England factories have resigned themselves to allowing the children to remain completely away from the pious atmosphere of the mills. Thus has man's inventiveness placed new hazards in the paths of these little ones whose morals formerly were so well guarded by their fourteen-hour day under the benevolent eye of a Massachusetts foreman. Another mainstay of the professional reformers is not applicable to Cousin Charley's mill. No women are employed there on the night shift for the reason that plenty of men have always been at hand for that kind of work. Even the comparatively low wages of the cotton mills have been like manna from the skies to those habituated to the incomes of tenant farmers.

4

Purely from the labor point of view, the current problem of the cotton industry is not so much related to the working conditions of women and children as it is to the question of whether the introduction of new machines will not gradually remove the necessity for any kind of unskilled labor—children, women, or men. In the modern

kraft paper mills of the South unskilled workers even
now are employed only in a few minor departments. At
Muscle Shoals three or four highly trained men walk
about looking at gauges and charts in a room three hundred yards long. This gargantuan temple of the machine
contains a row of enormous softly humming dynamos,
and no unskilled workmen. But unskilled laborers are
not significant as purchasers of kraft paper bags and electrical energy. They do, however, buy cotton goods to
such an extent that they constitute the most important
market for that product. This fact Cousin Charley knows.
Experience has taught him that his mills are least profitable during periods of low-priced cotton; buying raw
materials cheaply in no sense compensates for the purchasing power lost by farmers with reduced incomes.

Thus he has been able to derive the most salient point
of his industrial philosophy: that the cotton mills are especially linked with agriculture in the South. While he
knows that machines do not pay fees to labor unions, he
also realizes that machines have no purchasing power. In
many respects he would agree with the essentials of
Henry Pratt Fairchild's essay entitled "Machines Don't
Buy Goods." The money Cousin Charley pays for raw
materials goes directly to the cotton farmer, and part of
the wages earned in the mills is sent by employees to their
relatives who are still eating corn meal and "white meat"
on their rented patches of sterile land. These principles

were not taught Cousin Charley by Henry Ford or Stuart Chase, although he has books by these gentlemen in his library. Apparently Cousin Charley is nearer to reality than is either Henry Ford or Stuart Chase. He is not exploiting the advertising power of a high-flown theory; he is at grips with a fact. His nostrils remember the flavor of the fundamental earth.

As we walked along past the aisles of spindles in the mill, my mind fell into making a comparison of them with rows of cotton plants in the black belt. The men and women working at the whirring machines would in most cases have been in a cotton field at that moment, had the factories not been constructed in the South. Cousin Charley and I might have been riding horseback over the fields in the hot sunshine. The workers would have been mainly Negroes. Here in the mill Negroes were employed only at the heavy work of lifting the bulk cotton, in firing the furnaces, or in shifting multicolored batches of cotton in the dyeing room. White laborers would not have had much chance in the black belt; they would have eked out a sorry living in the red-clay lands farther north. In Cousin Charley's mill villages their food was better, more plentiful, and more varied. Under expert instruction in the villages, the women kept their houses neat and made simple dresses for themselves from the mill cloth. Their children attended school nine months a year, instead of having, at best, in the country a short term and a teacher herself scarcely advanced from illiteracy. Milk, so frequently considered, on the tenant farms, a diet only for sick children, was to be had at extremely low prices from the mill dairy. Screened windows and foot coverings alleviated the ravages of malaria and hookworm.

The mill workers threw themselves into simple recreations with a hunger born of their former isolation and weariness of soul and body. At band concerts, at baseball games, at children's exercises that sparkling attention in their eyes was something new for many of these refugees from the barren hills. Lyrics sung about the peace and liberty of the countryside are not inspired by visits to the tenant farms from which these people had moved to factory town. Called upon by agents of the labor unions, Cousin Charley has them conducted through the mills and villages and then asks whether the union could do more for the employees than he himself has already done.

Still the metamorphosis of the mill people was not complete. Most of the women continued to sweep their front yards with brooms, giving them the appearance of those in little Dutch villages, and to scour their house floors with stiff brushes and lye soap. The waltz and two-step could not supplant the old-fashioned square dance in the favor of the older couples. And Cousin Charley explained to me that all the floor corners in the mill were painted white so as to place a special burden upon the conscience of the employees whose rural habit of chewing tobacco continued to survive in spite of every other sort of tactful discouragement. On the whole, I could not help wondering what Jean Jacques Rousseau would conclude, should he be able to compare a tenant farmer's hillside shack with one of the company houses at Cousin Charley's mill; and whether Irving Babbitt, after a similar experience, would be constrained to add a footnote to his *Rousseau and Romanticism*.

5

But on our tour of inspection Cousin Charley did not become truly excited until we had ridden out to his chicken farm about a mile from the mill. My knowledge of chickens is not exhaustive, but a flock of five hundred white leghorn pullets must be one of the memorable scenes of chickendom, unless it be eclipsed by the sight of eight hundred fluffy yellow leghorns at the age of four days.

An hour previously I had watched a Swiss dyer stand guard over the mysteries of his secret process in the mills. From a tub of liquid, strips of denim cloth had risen into the air over a system of rollers. Going up it was green; coming down it was blue. Somewhere in the air, oxidation had taken place. The Swiss dyer had brought his secrets from Europe, where his father had passed them on to him orally from his grandfather. He was austere and rather forbidding of countenance. Polite he was, to be sure; but even his deference to Cousin Charley did not conceal his suspicion that one of us might catch a sample of that mysterious dyeing liquid in a test tube. Cousin Charley knew that ownership of the mills ten times over would never disclose to him the exact nature of the dyeing process which he had imported from Switzerland.

Much the same was true of the custodian of the chickens, Mr. Pollette, whom Cousin Charley had brought from England. Mr. Pollette was anything but austere; he was the soul of enthusiasm and cordiality. But there remained certain details about the breeding of leghorns and the selection of eggs which he discussed only with an amiable wave of the hand and a very agreeable chuckle. At the dairy farm situated near by Cousin Charley had placed a Wisconsin expert in charge of his fine Jersey and Hereford cattle.

Near the cattle barns Cousin Charley had set out three acres of shrubbery upon which he was experimenting. Feeling the texture of its leaves, prodding about the stalks of it with a small stick, standing off and gazing appraisingly upon its coloration, he gave the clear impression of having forgotten entirely that he was the owner of a vast array of machinery which puffed and fumed less than a mile away. In that mill were many hundreds of southern tenant farmers but lately changed into industrial workers. Under Cousin Charley's sympathetic encouragement, some of them might hope to be advanced from spinners to weavers, from foremen perhaps to superintendents. Such things had frequently occurred. But they never might hope to be dyers, chicken raisers, cattle breeders, or horticulturists. These positions Cousin Charley reserved for the elect of God.

Remarkably enough, all the mills in Cousin Charley's group have been able to maintain very nearly a full-time schedule regardless of the depression and the competition of the mushroom growth of migratory factories which sprang up as a result of the boom. His industries were established long before the southern factory boom of the 1920's; partly as a consequence of that fact, they have not been ruined by a recession from the hysteria of business inflation. During the peak of commercial prosperity Cousin Charley saw no cause for employing the stretch-out system in his mill; and now at low tide his regular families are conservatively pursuing their accustomed work. On their southern plantations the ancestors of Cousin Charley had become habituated to the responsibility of caring sympathetically for the needs of hundreds of unresourceful dependents. This predetermined attitude toward his employees Cousin Charley carried with him into industry. Whatever evils a system of paternalism may cause in thwarting the development of individual traits among the employed, those evils can-

Picketing at a paper mill strike.

The machine age overtakes a beautiful old southern mansion of Italian Renaissance architecture.

not be suffered by people who need a strong arm to lean
upon considerably more than they need new worlds to
conquer. Without laboring the point, it is sufficient to
say that native paternalism is a pearl of great price as com-
pared with the savageries of outside exploitation.

The question rises as to whether Cousin Charley's mill
is typical of the southern cotton factories of today. Only
a cursory examination of certain regions of botched civilization in the South at this moment is necessary to demonstrate that Cousin Charley's factory is on a different plane
from many of the others. Some of the lamentable results
of the intrusion of the machine below the Potomac are
matched only by the depravities of life in some of the
poorer rural sections of the South before the factories
came. But Cousin Charley's mill is definitely representative of a certain class of native industrial development
in the southern region. In several states of the South there
are families which have turned sturdily from the plantation to the factory without altering one jot the desirable
elements of their cultural inheritance. Similarly, other
families have turned from plantation life to the lumber
industry within recent years. Had Cousin Charley lived
in a more fertile and more traditional southern state than
the one in which he does live—and had there been fewer
industrial resources easily at hand—I have no doubt that
he at this moment would be serenely and properly en-

sconced upon many green acres as a country squire. But who will say that in his present capacity he is less useful to civilization?

It was not until we had passed the obdurate cast-iron rabbit on Cousin Charley's smooth wide lawn that I remembered that balance sheets, bills of lading, and production charts had not been mentioned during our inspection of his mill. Such an omission, I felt, was strange in a giant of industry, and most delightfully characteristic of Cousin Charley. But when we had gone into his white house and seated ourselves for afternoon coffee in little Spode cups, he turned with a somewhat harassed and injured expression on his face. "Look here," said Cousin Charley. "It's that man Pollette. Now do you really think he ought to wear those black and white checked breeches out in that chicken yard?"

Chapter X

The Philosopher's Stone

I

As the alchemists of old are said to have sought for a preparation capable of changing the baser metals into purest gold, certain coteries of southerners today appear to be searching for a magic formula—or perhaps an opiate—by means of which the disagreeable problems of the South may be caused to vanish from their consciousness, leaving there only visions of a Utopia far more elegant and refined than anything Sir Thomas More dared hope for as he dreamed in sixteenth-century England. Although such dreams are not without their enchantment, I cannot escape the conviction that southerners would have a better chance to find the philosopher's stone by opening their eyes than they would by keeping them tightly closed.

When one is eating blue point oysters and soft shell crabs in Baltimore, he is in no position to hold his own, either physically or mentally. The peculiar power of these delectable dishes quite overcomes his resistance. Much the same may be said of the food served in the celebrated restaurants of New Orleans; but the New Orleans people are not so much inclined to talk about "significant" subjects as are the Baltimoreans. Therefore, let a southerner be on his guard when he converses over luncheon tables in Baltimore, for there is always the danger that certain heterodox opinions may enter his susceptible mind, to remain there constantly plaguing him for the rest of his days. I speak from experience. Once, rendered defenseless by blue point oysters and soft shell crabs in Baltimore, I found myself nodding assent to a couple of observations which I, as a good and hopeful southerner, should never, never have countenanced. The first was that Virginius Dabney's *Liberalism in the South* (containing 456 pages including the index) was entirely too long, because there simply never had been that much liberalism in the South. The second—and much worse—one was that southerners have no sense of discrimination. It was averred, as I recall, that southerners are extraordinarily weak in their ability to recognize a good man when they see one. This insult appeared to be based partly upon the South's willingness to allow so many of its most talented sons and daughters to migrate to other sections of the country, the while being content to glorify many other persons who obviously were shallow bounders and wind-bags. Again, it was charged that the South habitually marshaled all of its forces in a patriotic defense of itself against the pin-pricks of petty propagandists and other small fry from other parts of the country, while it chose to ignore the really salient and important criticisms levelled by its own serious thinkers, as well as those offered in good faith by informed and objective students living in other parts of the nation. In short, the consensus at the table was that the South, despite its reputation for lethargy, is constantly distinguishing itself by getting terrifically excited about the wrong things.

Recalling that conversation, I am faced by a dilemma. Should I attempt to confound these Maryland critics by addressing to them a brief but powerfully facetious note with reference to the savage mob spirit which enveloped their eastern shore region not long ago? Or should I capitulate by admitting that the present attitude towards the Scottsboro case in some sections of the South seems to be a clear illustration of the southerner's innate lack of discrimination?

The current report is that Samuel Leibowitz, the outstanding defense attorney in the Scottsboro case, has announced his withdrawal from the whole affair. The following statement is attributed to him: "The Communists have raised huge sums of money by exploitation of this case through paid admission to mass meetings throughout the country and kindred forms of lucrative ballyhoo." Referring to apparently well-supported charges that irresponsible propagandists have attempted to bribe the key witness, Mrs. Victoria Price, Mr. Leibowitz is quoted as having declared that he would resign as counsel unless all Communists were removed from the case. "The

events in Alabama in the past week," his printed statement continues, "have convinced me that there is no
other course left open. My defense has been hampered
by mysterious moves behind the scenes by the International Labor Defense." Yet, ludicrous as have been
some of the jealous tilts between the extremely radical
I.L.D., the more moderate National Association for the
Advancement of Colored People, and the various defense
attorneys who have claimed that their services have been
rendered without remuneration from any source, these
side-shows ought not to be allowed to blind the South
to the weighty questions which the Scottsboro case has
raised with reference to the jurisdiction of the thirteenth,
fourteenth, and fifteenth amendments in the southern
states.

If the South can show that these offensive Civil War
amendments are no more than an embodiment of the
malevolent hiss of such names as Stevens, Stanton,
Seward, and Sumner, then they should definitely go the
way of the eighteenth amendment, which a majority of
the American people now seem to have recognized as
the result of a mistaken zeal. If it can be demonstrated
that the Civil War amendments cannot be complied with,
in the light of social conditions which pertain in the
South, they should by all means be repudiated legally
and in a dignified manner. If, on the other hand, the principles which they contain can be shown to be in the

interest of a more humane and enlightened civilization
in the South, then they should be observed. Spontaneous
assumptions, not based upon consecrated and profound
study of conditions, have no validity on either side. At
any rate, the South should have discrimination enough
to be able to realize what the issues actually are, conscience enough to wish to do what is just, and courage
enough to see the problem through in the sight of God
and man.

2

The South is extraordinarily sensitive to criticism—no
doubt too much so for its own good. This over-sensitive-
ness probably is largely due to the defense mechanisms
which naturally were built up in the southern mind during the reckless and reprehensible looting of the southern
province which took place after the assassination of Abraham Lincoln, and which the sincere but yielding Andrew
Johnson could not prevent. It must be remembered that
much of the temper of present-day thought in the South
is under the influence of aged Confederates whose souls
were tinged with justifiable bitterness during the unspeakably cruel and conscienceless reign of vengeance
which the North allowed to hold sway in the South after
the Civil War—a vengeance far more terrible and relentless than that inflicted upon any other conquered nation
in modern times—one which makes the Treaty of Ver-

sailles appear sweet and Christian by comparison. Yet, what of the younger generations in the South? Are they to assume that there are three kinds of culture in the world: artistic or scholarly, sociological, and southern—and that, of these three, the southern culture is the only one worth a second thought?

The South must decide whether its best interests are always served by that backward vision which, for want of a better characterization, is termed traditionalism. Evidence seems to indicate that, at least in a few specific instances, southern people have tended to deprive themselves of definite advantages by cleaving to an unimaginative reliance upon an established way of life. A vivid illustration of such a case is furnished by some of the experiences which the Tennessee Valley Authority has had in its efforts to raise cultural standards and to lower the cost of living in certain sections of Tennessee and Alabama.

Although it stands within a stone's cast of the Woodrow Wilson dam at Muscle Shoals, Florence is the most conspicuous of the North Alabama towns which have rather suspected that the TVA program represents a second reconstruction and that its northern executives are really carpet-baggers but thinly disguised as social planners. The Alabama Florentines, to be sure, at last succumbed to the temptations of cheap government power. Even so, the reasons for their long delay in doing so are of sufficient import to deserve a place in the record.

Florence's indignation against the TVA rests principally upon two counts, both of which have to do with land. Dr. Arthur E. Morgan has scotched the real-estate speculators in the Muscle Shoals district, and he is quoted as having declared that most of the agricultural land in the Tennessee Valley, because it has been so consistently mistreated from the days of slavery down to the present time, is worth no more than about $25 an acre. While Dr. Morgan's admirable campaign against the land-sharks has caused chagrin at Muscle Shoals, his adverse rating of land values in the vicinity of Florence has caused descendants of the ante-bellum squirearchy in that region to burn with anguish, and to talk among themselves about "insults," with the connotation of outrageous persecution which the unreconstructed southerner has packed into that expression. For anyone, especially a "Yankee" from Ohio, to intimate that their river bottom land has been ruined through slipshod and ignorant methods of cultivation is not merely a shock in an economic sense; far worse than that, it virtually is tantamount to an insult to their grandfathers. Among themselves, however, the Tennessee Valley landowners do not hesitate to admit that soil erosion, the lack of fertilizer, and the reliance upon a one-crop system have played havoc with the actual values of their property. But this realization has the effect of adding color to their quixotic measures in forcing TVA to condemnation proceedings. One old planter of the region is particularly well known because of the caustic remarks which he used to make with reference to the gullies and red-clay banks in the middle of his fields. Comparing his Alabama domain to a portion of Kentucky which he loved, he would remark that, if the inhabitants of the blue-grass section had treated their land as badly as farmers of the Tennessee Valley had treated theirs, "crows would have to carry their rations to fly over it." This old realist always used to conclude his tirades by declaring, "If I hadn't been a southerner, I would have been an abolitionist." Such heresies are permitted southerners when their temperament becomes separated from their sectional loyalty. But similar aberrations on the part of the president of an Ohio college, sent to represent what might be regarded as absentee landlords in Washington, conjured up ghosts of carpet-bag days.

A short while ago the TVA announced a proposal to buy the existing electrical distribution facilities serving thirteen north Alabama communities, and in turn to sell this equipment to each of the towns on a plan which would enable them to enjoy the benefits of cheap electricity while they were paying for their municipal plants over a ten-year period. Twelve of the communities promptly acceded to this program. Florence alone stalled and demurred. For several weeks it was not able to make up its mind, although citizens of the town convened in mass meetings and much oratory was heard pro and con. Only the most superficial analysis would attribute the delay at Florence wholly, or even primarily, to any sinister anti-TVA influence of the Alabama Power Company (in which I own three shares of preferred stock). The truth is that Florence appeared to have the jitters. As the background used by T. S. Stribling in *The Store* and *Unfinished Cathedral*, one of which won a Pulitzer prize and the other of which was a Literary Guild selection, the town was sure for a time that it had a new appreciation of the way General Lee's soldiers felt after Appomattox. From what it heard about Carl Carmer's *Stars Fell on Alabama* (another Literary Guild selection), Florence was not unwilling to believe that the whole United States had lined up actively on Mr. Stribling's side. Hence it is no wonder that Dr. Morgan was kept waiting for a time.

As the TVA moved in and acquired extensive holdings at what the landowners often considered unjustifiably low prices, natives of the lower end of the Tennessee Valley—remaining under the spell of their traditional culture—foresaw their own eclipse. Descendants of the pioneers, who insisted that whatever development may have taken place was the result of their plantation economy, they could see no future for themselves in a land dedicated to small units of agriculture and industry—

primarily for the benefit of the people of the lower middle class. Therefore, remembering a story which the President of the United States used to tell about hunting in Cuba when he was assistant secretary of the Navy, they unveiled their contempt by characterizing the TVA as "Mr. Roosevelt's great shrink bird." Or, changing the figure, they expressed their passive dismay by saying, "The TVA has its foot on our neck."

Although the vigorous newspapers of the Muscle Shoals district (the Florence *Herald*, the Tuscumbia *Times* and the Sheffield *Standard*) at first showed a tendency to launch complaints and adverse criticisms at the TVA, they later were extremely influential in the building of a public opinion fully appreciative of the advantages which the government was attempting to bring to their region. But the real-estate operators remained unforgiving in their attitude towards Dr. Morgan. Florence has dreamed for more than a hundred years that its river would some day make it a great city. Strangers hear of the first land sales in the early years of the last century, when James Madison and Andrew Jackson bought lots; of the boom of the eighties; of the World War activities and of Henry Ford's offer to build a city seventy-five miles long and employing a million people. The failure of Dr. Morgan to give solidity to pipe dreams of this category came as a devastating anticlimax to the lack of interest shown by three Republican presidents. Nor did the boosters of the region like Dr. Morgan's statement that Florence should never expect to support a permanent population of more than 25,000. That, to the real-estate promoters—both native and imported—was the final straw!

Therefore, in the face of the antagonism resulting from a strange conglomeration of boosterism and traditionalism, the TVA was forced to exercise a considerable amount of patience and tact before it could deliver to the Tennessee Valley the gifts prepared at the instigation of the only president of the United States who has shown any special and imaginative interest in the South within the memory of this generation.

3

I think it reasonable to conclude that we southerners have been too prone to magnify the not wholly flattering opinions of outsiders during recent years; that we who were born long after the Civil War have too easily accepted the conviction that the rest of the country is against us, when, as a matter of fact, the rest of the country has been pretty well involved with its own serious problems. A few years ago I wrote a note to a native of Michigan who, after sojourning in the South for a period of years during which he contributed handsomely to the cultural life of this region, had returned to his native state. In reply to my inquiry as to whether he was going to continue his interests in southern life, he wrote about as follows: "Unfortunately I find my time taken up by a new set of university courses, and myself among people who know little and care less about the South; so I shall probably not be thinking much more in terms of that far-away land which so interested and charmed me when I lived there." The people residing elsewhere in the United States are decidedly less concerned with the problems of the South than southerners sometimes suppose. After all, the burden of determining the future of this region is one which southern people must take upon their own shoulders.

Again, there are thoughtful northerners who profess the highest opinion of the potentialities of the southern character. Not long ago I was in Madison, Wisconsin, talking with Philip F. La Follette. This young American revolutionary did not know I was from the South, since I was interviewing him as a representative of the New York *Times*. But, ruminating on the possibilities of a political alignment between the agricultural interests of the Middle West and those of the South, he said he liked southerners, that he had always believed in them—that southerners had what he called "guts." From the La Follette point of view, this younger son of "Old Fighting Bob" could not have paid a more heartfelt compliment to the South. My own feeling is that this tribute to southern boldness and audacity was entirely deserved, but that southerners frequently have failed to exert their courage in the direction best calculated to gain the ends demanded by considerations of social welfare in the broadest sense.

Riding today over the rich and beautiful Wisconsin countryside, which gives the impression of being a natural park stretching for mile after mile through gently undulating pasture lands of thick grass, or walking beneath the fine elms and oaks of gem-like cities such as Madison, the white stone buildings of which gleam on a peninsula between two lakes, one may imagine that he is conscious of the natural and cultural forces which made possible the rise of the La Follette progressivism in that state during the final decade of the past century. Wisconsin impresses a visitor with its fertility, its strength, its changeableness, its rugged democracy. Everybody says "Hello." Over most of the best dairy country of Wisconsin last summer the heavy Guernsey and Hereford cattle could be seen fattening on grass as succulent and green as ever it was before the sun ravaged the grazing lands of Minnesota, the Dakotas, and Wyoming. The comfortable and impeccably kept farmhouses, painted red or white, with their enormous stock barns and silos for hay and grain, with their brilliantly colored flowers sparkling on front lawns clipped as smooth as billiard tables, did not suggest either depression or drought. Nor would one be likely to think of social revolution in connection with such houses. Rather, one would be reminded of the remark of a traveler who said that the contentedness and air of well-being about the Wisconsin countryside is the very embodiment of what the Germans call *Gemütlichkeit*.

Yet, the strength of the hearty Wisconsin people is such that they are never satisfied. They have much; but, stirred by their own vigor, they are determined to have more. This urge towards change, it has been said by those who know the region well, is motivated partly by the unusual variations in climatic conditions. You might retire on a hot August night and wake up the next morning to find comfort in woolen clothing and perhaps a sweater; whereupon the natives say, "It's a little *fresh* today." Or you might be motoring along a smooth gravel road, half asleep in the warm sunshine, when the wind will suddenly start blowing steadily and with such force as to make it difficult for you to keep your automobile on the highway. In the winter months, balmy weather may be supplanted in a few hours by a blizzard which blows the dry snow in clouds, as if it were powdered chalk, and leaves a temperature of twenty degrees below zero under a cheerful sun. This tremendous energy of the weather, one is led to believe, has its influence upon the mental and physical vitality of the people. Their personalities demand change—improvement—in the social, political and economic aspects of their lives. It is not by accident, for instance, that the state law allows the Wisconsin peo-

ple to change governors every two years, and that they
usually do so. In such a soil La Follette liberalism—or
radicalism, if one wishes to call it that—was bound to
flourish.

My purpose is not to suggest any invidious comparisons between Wisconsin and the southern states. I, for
one, would far rather live in the South—for all its faults—
than in any other part of the world that I have ever seen.
But, as I attempted to say at the outset, the southern
climate does have the effect of creating a passivity which
renders the inhabitants of the region much too willing to
accept conditions as they are, be they right or wrong.
Coupled with this physical passivity in the southern people, there is a vast and cumbersome array of traditionalism, which encourages an outlook compounded of
partly mythological assumptions and criteria unable to
stand the test of reasonable analysis. The result is that the
South for too long has been dominated by a divagating
emotionalism and a willingness to be satisfied with the
second best in both material and intellectual accomplish-
ments.

On the whole, the South would profit from a nice,
quiet revolution. I do not mean a Communistic revolt,
or another Populist uprising, or further developments of
Fascism in the South—may the good Lord deliver us from
all such things as those! What I have in mind is a revision
of the region's implanted ideas, a clarification of issues,

a realistic and direct recognition of existing social problems, a redirection of the South's courage and audacity, and a determination that the southern conscience shall be accorded the reverence due a sacred thing. Sweet placidity, although it is a gem of great value, must not be purchased at the expense of the southerner's moral responsibility for the welfare of the social structure below the Potomac. Those who love the Old South may take their choice of courses: they may either exist in complacent dreams, hoping that they will not too soon be cast from their beds by a sudden rocking of the earth beneath them; or they may resolve to wrestle with substantial problems with all the strength and skill at their command, inspired by another kind of vision—one which leads them to hope that the present and future of the South may yet prove worthy of the glamorous reputation of the ante-bellum years.